The Man Who Discovered the Amazon

The Man Who Discovered the Amazon

by RONALD SYME

illustrated by WILLIAM STOBBS

New York · WILLIAM MORROW & CO. · *1958*

Second Printing, August 1959

© 1958 by William Morrow and Company, Inc. All rights
reserved. Published simultaneously in the Dominion of
Canada by George J. McLeod Limited, Toronto. Printed
in the United States of America.

Library of Congress Catalog Card No. 58-5365

Contents

2120

The Man Who Discovered the Amazon

Chapter One

The Unknown Mountains

WESTWARD came the great ships of Spain. With square white sails and high-decked hulls, they swayed onward across the Atlantic Ocean.

The vessels were steering for the glittering green islands of the Caribbean Sea, which Christopher Columbus had discovered only thirty-five years before. Hard-eyed Spanish adventurers aboard the ships were dreaming already of the gold and land and slaves they might find on the western side of the Atlantic.

Among these soldiers of fortune was young and lanky Francisco de Orellana. He was scarcely out of his teens, and therefore a little shy in the swaggering company of his fellow passengers. Secretly he wondered how he would fare in the hard and dangerous times which lay ahead. These other men with him had already seen and done so much. They had fought in European wars and against the Moors in North Africa. Some of them had already crossed the Atlantic more than once. All their past experience would help them greatly in the struggle to acquire wealth somewhere in the New World.

Orellana knew that this struggle was growing harder year by year. The earliest settlers from Spain had taken everything worth having in the islands of Cuba, Hispaniola (Haiti), Jamaica, and Puerto Rico. But beyond the western shores of the Caribbean Sea lay the vast country of Mexico, which Hernando Cortes had recently conquered for Spain. There were plenty of good acres to be found in Mexico. Men who had been there said there was also a certain amount of gold, and that the defeated Aztec Indians made obedient slaves.

Yet the land of Mexico was not for young Francisco de Orellana. When he had come aboard this ship in Spain, he had thought of going there. But by keeping his ears open, he had heard the passengers discussing a soldier-explorer named Francisco Pizarro, who was seeking men to sail southward with him and join in the conquest of the mysterious Inca kingdom of Peru.

There was no great enthusiasm for that idea among the veterans with Orellana. Pizarro was looking for ships in Panama, and the little vessels in that port were mostly worm-holed and unseaworthy. Anyone who sailed in them was risking his life long before he ever reached Peru. Yet, without knowing why, Orellana had already decided to become one of Pizarro's volunteers just as soon as he could reach the settlement of Panama. Eagerly he listened to conversations about Pizarro and the forthcoming expedition.

The veteran soldiers aboard saw that Orellana was interested in what they were saying. They glanced amusedly at his solemn face and lean figure, or watched him trying awkwardly to stroll up and down the heaving deck.

"There goes one with more imagination than

fighting skill," they murmured. "No doubt he has great ideas of winning a fortune for himself with his nice new sword. To look at him, one would say he might do better to stay at home with his books. Yet if he lives long enough, he will learn more than he could ever find in the greatest libraries of Spain."

The veterans were right. Men who returned to Spain usually spoke only of the wealth, the fertile soil, and the warm sunshine of the New World. They seldom mentioned the deadly fevers of the mangrove swamps, or the bone-tipped arrows of Indian tribes. They seemed to forget about those comrades whose frozen bodies lay in high mountain passes, and others who had died of hunger in silent jungles. But no man who had visited the New World ever really forgot these grim experiences.

Orellana discovered all these hardships when he stepped ashore in Peru as a volunteer in Pizarro's little army. During the next twelve years he was content if he found shelter for the night, enough food to satisfy his hunger, and no immediate danger of death. Gradually he became an expert fighter with sword, lance, and crossbow. Other Spaniards began to say that Francisco de Orellana was one of the best officers, even though he seldom spoke more than a few words and showed a queer interest in the customs and language of the Inca people.

Peru was conquered at last. The Spaniards began squabbling among themselves over their share of gold and land and silver mines. Many of them turned on their old leader, Pizarro, and marched against him in rebellious battle.

Francisco de Orellana was not among these traitors. "When first I came to Peru," he said to Pizarro, "I promised to serve faithfully in your army. That promise still binds me. Win or lose, you remain my leader."

Orellana's reward came a year or two later. The mutinous army was smashed in battle and its leaders were dead, in prison, or hiding in the forests. Pizarro was a man who seldom forgot his enemies or friends. Now he was the all-powerful Viceroy of Peru.

"Go north to the province of Guayaquil," he told Orellana. "You shall be the governor of that district. There is as much land for you as any man could want. Off the coast there are pearl fisheries; in the hills there are emeralds. One fifth of all this wealth from the sea and the soil shall be yours; the rest is either the King of Spain's or mine. Take with you some good Spanish fighting men to protect the town you must build on the banks of the Guayas River; the Indian tribes of Guayaquil are enemies of ours."

Two years later, in 1540, Orellana had done his best to build a town. It was a mean and horrid place that stank of river mud and fever. The Spaniards lived in mud-brick huts, the Indian slaves in hovels built of straw. Yet now a high wooden palisade surrounded the place, and small ships came to anchor in the river. Scorpions and snakes, mosquitoes and bats, lurked in dark corners of the houses, but Orellana's iron-bound chests were filling with precious stones and glowing pearls. His men grumbled at the heat and the tropical rain, and complained about the hordes of stinging insects and the lack of civilized foods. But they, too, had found ways of making money, and there were slaves to wait on them from morning to night. They grumbled but stayed where they were.

Captain-General Francisco de Orellana was now thirty-five years old. He was taller than most Spaniards, who were usually short and wiry. Tropical sunshine and the climate of Guayaquil had yellowed his long, serious face. During some earlier battle he had lost an eye, and his face was scarred by the sword blade. Usually he spoke quietly and in a strangely gentle manner. A stranger might have mistaken him for a lawyer, or a priest in ordinary clothes. There would have been some excuse for such a mistake. Orellana remained quiet and studious by nature. He was one of the very few Spaniards who troubled to learn the languages of the tribes. Within two years he could speak the dialect of Guayaquil as fluently as the Indians themselves. With pen and notebook in hand, he would spend half the night talking to some native from the unknown regions which lay inland. A couple of days later, he had learned the man's own language.

"By knowing a stranger's native tongue, one can understand him much better," Orellana said to the few friends who knew him well enough to joke about his studies. "One can then treat him kindly as a friend, or fight him wisely as an enemy."

"But why trouble your mind with such matters?" asked the friends. "Surely, sire, your days of adventure are ended? Here in Guayaquil, hot and dreary though it is, you have wealth and high position. There will be no need for you to face fresh hardships in mountain and jungle as an adventurer in search of such things."

In reply, Orellana merely smiled. He swung round in his chair to gaze inland across the green coastal plain to the distant snowy peaks of the Cordilleras Mountains. This gigantic wall of rock stood cold and hard and silent across the eastern sky.

"What lies on the other side of yonder sierras?" he asked. "Are there not, perhaps, greater countries than even this Peru of ours? Have you not heard of El Dorado, the Gilded One? The native emperor who is said to be coated in fresh gold-dust daily from head to foot? Where is this great monarch's country? Does it exist, or was it created merely by the tongue of some imaginative liar? These are the questions I would like to answer before the fevers of Guayaquil destroy my health, or age stiffens my limbs."

During his two years in this little town of Guayaquil, Orellana gazed often with his one sound eye at those remote icy peaks. He went on steadily increasing his wealth and his great knowledge of Indian languages. In some strange way he seemed to know that they would help him one day to fulfill his dream.

Three hundred miles north of Guayaquil lay the old mountain city of Quito. Once it had been the home of Indian kings. Now it was held by a Spanish garrison and had become the northern end of Spain's new empire in Peru. The Governor of Quito was thirty-six-year-old Gonzalo Pizarro, a younger brother of Francisco Pizarro, the Viceroy of Peru.

Gonzalo was a wild, handsome, and fearless man. His skill with lance, sword, and the firearm known as an arquebus had made him famous throughout Peru. He was a magnificent horseman and a fine leader of men. But Gonzalo was also obstinate, impatient, and reckless. While Orellana merely dreamed of fresh exploration beyond the Cordilleras, Gonzalo decided to go there. He invited Orellana to visit him in Quito.

"Old friend, we shall go together in search of the Gilded One," Gonzalo said. "You and I, in company with the best Spanish fighting men we can find. Even if we fail to find this famous king, I have no doubt we will discover fresh lands of great wealth."

"You mean the cinnamon forests, perhaps," Orellana replied. "Yes, I have heard that there are great stretches of spice-bearing trees somewhere beyond the mountains. With all Spain crying out for cinnamon with which to flavor the dull foods and drink of her people, those forests would bring enormous wealth to the man lucky enough to find them."

"Then hasten back to your mud flats by the Guayas River," said Gonzalo. "Pick your men, arm them well, and rejoin me here as swiftly as possible. I shall await your return impatiently."

The Spaniards in Guayaquil numbered only sixty-odd men. Some of them would have to remain to protect the town against the hostile tribes of the surrounding plains. African slaves who had been brought to Peru from Hispaniola would also have to stay in Guayaquil. Only two of them could be spared for the journey. One was known as Panama, the other as Number Five. Panama was a small but sturdy little fellow, Number Five a big and powerful man.

"I can take only twenty-four fighting men," Orellana said to the eager Spaniards who clustered round him. "Armor and weapons you have, and horses I shall provide if I can. But they are scarce, gentlemen, and will cost five hundred dollars each. Captain Pizarro says he is mustering a force of three hundred Spaniards, of whom half will be cavalry. He also proposes taking four thousand Indian carriers and two thousand hogs to keep his troops well fed. What our own party lacks in numbers, we must make up for in quality. See to it, comrades, that we have no reason to be ashamed of our appearance."

Out through the gates of the town stockade Orellana led his men. Down to the river they went, to the heavy rafts of balsa wood awaiting them. Spaniards and horses, Indian bearers, baggage, and thirty fierce dogs were divided up among these big rafts. The two Negroes, Panama and Number Five, traveled with Orellana as his personal servants.

The damp greenery of the tropical jungle closed around the rafts as the Indians paddled up the muddy river. A glaring sun swung across the sky, and its scorching heat radiated from the shining surface of the water. The Spaniards stripped off the bright steel corselets which protected their bodies, and laid aside the morions which weighed heavily on their heads. With perspiration running off them, they lay on the rafts, slapping their exposed faces and hands continuously to drive off the swarms of insects.

For ten days, Orellana's men went on up that

steamy river. At sunset they moored the rafts to the bank, lit smoky fires which they hoped would keep away the insects, and ate supper. Afterwards they lay and sweltered under cotton sheets which protected their bodies from the blood-hungry mosquitoes.

On the eleventh day, they began their overland march to Quito, where Gonzalo Pizarro was awaiting them. Now they followed a twisting, narrow trail through the damp, stagnant heat of the jungle. They came to streams which had to be crossed by wading or swimming, or by marching across Indian bridges built of interwoven lianas, which swung and trembled alarmingly under the weight of men and horses.

Orellana studied the perspiring, mud-streaked faces of his men and their damp-rusted armor.

"Grumble not because your bodies are sweating," he advised them. "See, ahead of us the track is beginning to climb. We are nearing the foothills of the Cordilleras. In a few days from now you will remember sorrowfully the nights when you could sleep without shivering. I traveled this way when I went to see Captain Pizarro, and I know what I am saying."

The jungle thinned out and the last trees

vanished as the Spaniards climbed higher. They came to rocky mountain passes where scarcely a patch of grass was visible. Sometimes the road, which had been cut by Inca engineers of a bygone age, wound round the towering face of a cliff. From its outward edge to the green valleys below was a drop of several thousand feet. The horses sweated with terror, and the Spaniards muttered prayers as they led the animals along the treacherous surface. The temperature after sunset dropped far below freezing, and a terrible icy wind moaned through the passes.

Spaniards, Indians, horses, and dogs slept together in caves or deserted stone resthouses built by the Incas. They collected every scrap of firewood they could find, yet they shivered miserably around the fires they built at night. The Indians began to cough and die. They were accustomed to the hot climate of Guayaquil and could not stand the mountain cold.

Twenty-five Spaniards and the two hundred Indians who lived through the journey tramped into the little mountain town of Quito early in March, 1541.

The Incas who built Quito had made wide streets which they surfaced with slabs of stone.

The good houses in which they lived were now inhabited by Spanish settlers who had come to dwell in this lonely region. The sheltered valleys outside the town were filled with good earth, in which pineapples and mangoes, potatoes and granadillas, flourished in wonderful profusion. Quito was a pleasant little town, where the heat of the burning sun was cooled by the mountain breeze, and frequent showers washed the streets and refreshed the growing crops.

There was no sign of Gonzalo Pizarro and his three hundred Spaniards in Quito.

"The Captain was eager to begin his journey," a passing Spaniard explained to Orellana. "He left here more than a week ago to start searching for El Dorado. You, Captain Orellana, will have to return to Guayaquil with your little party, I fear."

Orellana peered at the man coolly. "Return, señor? Why?"

The man shrugged and pointed to the distant mountain peaks. "With only twenty-four fighting men you would never succeed in overtaking Captain Pizarro. Beyond the Cordilleras, where the road descends to the jungle, live fierce tribes of Indians. They may hesitate to attack Captain Pizarro's army, but they would most certainly destroy you and your little party. Those Indians have quaint tortures, Captain Orellana, including the use of bamboo splinters, red-hot stones, and fire. That is why I say you must go back to Guayaquil. I see you have only seventeen horsemen, four crossbowmen, and three fellows carrying arquebuses. You would not get far, Captain Orellana."

"Far enough to overtake my friend Pizarro, I hope," Orellana replied. He turned in the saddle and made a sign to his men to dismount. "We will remain for two days in Quito to rest after our journey through the mountains. Afterwards, we will march onward again. I promised Pizarro that I would join him as soon as possible. I do not make or break a promise very easily, my friend."

Chapter Two

The Forest March

IT WAS not hard to follow Pizarro's trail across the mountains. The skeletons of dead Indian porters lay beside the road. There were also cold ashes and blackened patches of ground where campfires had once burned.

Orellana drove his men fast and mercilessly. "We will march every day from dawn till nearly dusk," he said. "We have less than two hundred Indian bearers now, and if we delay in these mountains, the rest of them will die of cold. Every slave who falls by the roadside means a loss to us of fifty pounds of supplies. I do not intend to sacrifice gunpowder, arrows for crossbows, and lead for bullets. We shall go short of food, my friends, but not of the weapons we need to fight with. Therefore we must pass through these mountains as swiftly as possible."

A horse slipped over the edge of a precipice and fell, screaming pitifully, to its death in the jungle far below the trail. The poor Indians of the warm coastal plains, their bodies thinly protected against the cold, collapsed and died. The Spaniards were forced to dismount from their horses and walk all day to keep from being frozen. Over their suits of armor they wore padded cotton jackets, three inches thick, which gave extra protection against Indian arrows. Hungry dogs slunk along miserably with tails tucked between their legs. Ever-watchful vultures soared unceasingly back and forth in the pale blue sky, waiting for the next Indian that would be left behind. Orellana, his face pinched and blue with cold, moved back and forth along the plodding line of men to hurry and encourage them. "We must be overtaking

Pizarro," he said. "No army the size of his could move as fast as we can. We'll be out of these accursed mountains and down in the jungle before long, *compañeros*. Down among the mosquitoes, the vampire bats, and the heat! Let's enjoy this good cold air while we can, even though it makes our bones ache. It will toughen us for what lies ahead. . . . Ho, Alonso Garcia! Turn back, I pray you, and see what causes those Indians to delay. The foolish fellows appear almost eager to die."

Round the last bend in the mountain road Orellana led his plodding, shivering men. They raised their cold-inflamed eyes to see what fresh miseries lay ahead of them. Their bearded faces became more cheerful, and they began to trudge a little faster. A few even managed to utter jests.

Far below, and in front of the plodding men, a great green sea of jungle reached to the horizon. Already the wind seemed to be losing a little of its deadly sharpness and to bring a slight fragrance of flowers and rain-wet vegetation. The Spaniards knew then that they were through the mountains. In front of them lay a vast and unknown country where no European had yet set foot. According to legend, somewhere in this enormous land was the empire of El Dorado and those priceless forests of cinnamon trees. And by the bones and broken straps on the road, the men knew they still followed the path taken by Gonzalo Pizarro.

For several days the Spaniards had been living mainly on boiled maize. But on the day they emerged from the icy gloom of the mountain passes, they shot large rabbits with crossbows which could throw an arrow accurately for two hundred yards. That night they ate rabbit stew mixed with a sweet-tasting root they dug out of the earth. When they awoke next morning, there was no ice on their beards, nor was their drinking water frozen solid.

Indian war parties attacked them that day. The warriors appeared from among scattered groves of trees which grew in the thin mountain soil. The dark-skinned, almost naked savages were armed with slings, throwing spears, and stone-headed axes. Yelling and jumping with excitement, several hundred of these Indians lined up across the downward path.

Orellana rode forward alone to meet them. Gradually the shouting and whooping subsided. In curious silence the Indians looked at the lean solitary figure approaching them. They examined his face, searching in vain for an expression of fear, and exclaimed with amazement when Orellana spoke to them in their own language.

"We have not come here to fight you," he called. "We merely wish to overtake our comrades, whom you must have seen passing through your country."

For a few moments the crowd of warriors swayed uncertainly back and forth. Above the voices of those who urged listening to what else this white stranger had to say, rose the yells and cries of those in favor of attacking the Spaniards. Abruptly the Indians charged up the slope at the little party of mailclad men.

Every Spaniard was a fighter. Shoulder to shoulder they waited until the Indians were upon them, and then they went into action. Fire-hardened wooden spears glanced uselessly off steel armor; primitive clubs were slashed in half by sharp-edged swords. The cavalry charged through the Indians, then wheeled about and charged again. The dogs took part in the fighting. They were large, long-haired, and savage brutes, trained to this kind of work. They slashed with ferocious teeth at the nearest Indians.

The Spaniards fought with wild courage. The battle swayed back and forth along the mountain slope. A horse fell, pierced to the heart by a thrusting spear, and his rider crashed to the ground. He was rescued by other Spaniards before the Indians could club him to death. Then a second horse went down. Once again the half-stunned rider was dragged to safety.

The fight lasted half an hour. All at once the Indians turned and ran for the nearest clump of trees, where low branches protected them from the horsemen. Yelling with fury, they watched Orellana and his followers go marching on down the mountain road.

Four more horses died of wounds that night, and several of the Spaniards were so weak from loss of blood that they could scarcely ride or walk. In those days there were no bandages, disinfectants, or drugs with which to treat injuries. The Spaniards merely strapped cloth pads over their wounds and allowed them to heal as best they could.

"If one handles hot coals, one must expect scorched fingers," Orellana said grimly, when he looked at his battered little army the next morning. "I do not think, however, that the

Indians will attack us again in open country. Come, the sun is up. We must start our day's march."

They reached the jungle and tramped into it. Although they were still following the trail made by Pizarro, swift-growing vegetation was already spreading across it again. A number of Indian porters transferred their loads to the remaining horses and started clearing a fresh path with long-bladed cutlasses. It was exhausting labor. During that day and the next, the Spaniards covered a total distance of only fourteen miles.

They came to the first of a number of rivers, which they crossed on a narrow but strong bridge built of lianas as thick as a ship's mooring hawser. Next came a deep and narrow river where the water roared between sheer walls of rock. Swinging their axes, Spaniards and Indians felled a number of trees to bridge the stream. By rolling the fallen trunks until they lay side by side, they built a trackway on which the nervous horses could cross.

"The rivers rose and fell with great rapidity," Orellana wrote in his diary. "We came to places where Captain Pizarro's men had crossed without getting wet above the knees, but we were out of our depth in the water. In other places we walked across a stream beside a bridge which Pizarro had been forced to build."

The little Negro, Panama, and his burly friend, Number Five, helped greatly with the construction of these bridges. They were the two best swimmers in Orellana's party. With light cords knotted around their waists, they often swam a wild torrent and then hauled across heavier lianas with which to lay the foundation of a new bridge that would dangle from side to side.

Despite all the care and courage of the Spaniards, they lost another of their precious horses while fording a river. The poor brute, already weakened from injuries and a shortage of proper food, was swept away by the current and drowned. Only nine horses now remained alive. Orellana worried about this. He knew that Indians feared Spanish cavalry more than anything else. When they faced men without horses, they fought with much greater fury and determination.

By this time the rain forest had become so thick that the Spaniards marched through a continuous green twilight. The matted foliage of the great trees above their heads completely shut out the sun and the sky. Droves of monkeys, parrots, and baboons squawked and yelled in the high tangle of leaves and branches, but remained almost invisible. Although the Spaniards were growing short of food, even their quickest and straightest-shooting crossbowmen and arquebusiers seldom got a chance to shoot any of these creatures. Indeed, the clumsy firearms were becoming almost useless. The hot, damp air of the jungle and the tropical rain had moistened the gunpowder. Moreover, Orellana was worried lest the supply of steel bolts for the crossbows would give out. There was no sign of the Indians, but drums beat continually in the jungle. The Spaniards knew that the savages were watching them all the time.

They came to a river which Pizarro had crossed on a bridge of lianas. The water ran with such speed and fury that great rocks and stones in its bed trundled downstream, making a continuous muttering roar as they rolled over and over. A mist of fine spray hung above the current, and the noise of the river was so frightful that the Spaniards had to shout to make themselves heard.

Jungle Indians had almost destroyed the bridge. Only two cables were left. These ran across the stream, one above the other and five feet apart.

Orellana glanced from the torrent to Number Five and Panama.

Both Negroes shook their heads.

"Captain," Number Five said gently, "if my friend and I try to swim across this river, we will not reach the other side. This is a matter of little importance to you, perhaps, but you will lose two men who can carry loads, help you to build other bridges, and fight when necessary."

"A sensible remark," Orellana said approvingly. He looked at his countrymen. "A man with strong hands and steady nerves might walk across on one liana if he held tightly to the one above it," he said. "I would go first myself, but it is my duty as leader to remain here in command of our horses and baggage, and to protect them if necessary until a bridge is made. I ask for volunteers to walk across the stream, taking fresh cables to the other side."

Alonso de Robles, a soft-spoken but courageous man, was the first to try. Diego Bermudez, a brown-faced, grinning seaman, went next. After him came two others. All four men were pale and trembling by the time they reached the opposite bank, but with them came the necessary lianas. Before nightfall, three new cables, lashed side by side, formed a new footbridge. Waist-high above it ran two more cables by which a man could steady himself.

Orellana thought it would take too long to build a bridge over which the horses could be led. He ordered them to be slung from a crude pulley arrangement and hauled across the river. The Spaniards kindled bonfires and went on working after darkness by the yellow glare of the flames.

The cables sagged dangerously under the weight of each horse. Their hoofs dangled only a few feet above the wild surface of the river. They screamed and struggled and were half-mad with terror by the time they were drawn ashore on the farther side.

Five horses and six Spaniards were across the stream when a bamboo trumpet sounded in the darkness of the jungle, and Indian warriors rushed to attack Orellana.

The fight surged back and forth in the firelight of the little clearing. A horse that had been dangling in midstream came ashore, dead from the javelins which had pierced its body. A heavy wooden drum started pounding in the forest, and the Indian trumpet went on blowing dismal blasts. Horses whinnied in fright, dogs barked with fury, and the Indians screamed their unceasing war cries. Thrown spears came whistling through the air, bruising or wounding Orellana and some of his men. A horse broke loose, bounded into the forest, and was stabbed to death. Another, wounded by a javelin, plunged into the river below.

"Get the Indian bearers across," shouted Orellana. "We must stand here until the last of them has reached the other side."

The porters, stooping under their heavy loads, hurried along the bridge. Some of them were ordered to tie sacks around their necks, containing the dogs. They were sure-footed men and they crossed swiftly. After them came the Spaniards, fighting until the last moment, when they were forced to grasp the steadying lianas. Orellana came last, while javelins and slingstones rattled continuously against his armor. The Indians began to surge across the bridge behind him. They were so numerous that they resembled a swarm of black ants crawling along a strip of wickerwork.

Orellana stepped ashore and looked back. The nearest Indian was almost across the river, and the lianas were sagging under the weight of many others.

"Cut the cables," he said.

Eager sword blades slashed through the lianas. The bridge swayed and fell. Scores of warriors plunged into the wild-running stream and were swept away into the darkness beyond the firelight.

Twenty-five Spaniards, the six remaining horses, and fifty Indians plodded onward through the shadowy tunnel of the jungle track. Panama and Number Five walked in their usual position by Orellana's side. Although they had stayed with him until the last moment during the fight at the bridge, neither of the Negroes was injured in any way.

Later that day, more Indians attacked from the thick undergrowth beside the track. At the same moment, a horse carrying a wounded Spaniard fell into a carefully hidden pit and was killed by sharp-pointed stakes placed in an upright position.

The fight was short but intense. The Indians fled back into the jungle without having killed or injured a Spaniard. The dead horse was skinned and its flesh divided into loads for the porters to carry. In the stagnant jungle air, meat of any kind soon became rotten. The Spaniards roasted as much as they could eat that night, gave the Indians a generous share, and fed the dogs. They threw away the rest, knowing that it would be uneatable by the following morning. After that they were left to face hunger again, for they had little to eat in their stores.

The whole forest was alive with Indians. Sometimes a warrior would leap out of the jungle, hurl a spear at the nearest Spaniard, and dive back into cover again. Others dug pits which they covered with branches and leaves, but the dogs nearly always gave warning of such pitfalls by growling and showing their teeth. Drums sent messages to other Indians ahead, and the tiny villages which the Spaniards passed through were always deserted and empty of food.

The men became weaker, and as their bodily strength decreased, their wounds started to fester. Some of the worst cases had to be carried on litters. Others insisted on walking, although they were suffering great pain. Food remained desperately hard to find; in all that lonely forest there seemed to be nothing a hungry man could eat.

When they came to a spot where Pizarro's army had encamped for the night, Orellana studied the cold ashes of the fires. "How long ago were they burning?" he asked one of the Indians.

The man peered at the ground. "Not more than three days ago," he said. "The sap has not yet dried completely on this broken branch, nor has new grass grown here where the fire burned brightest."

The Indians had also attacked Pizarro's men. In a clearing beside the trail, Orellana came to a destroyed village. Twenty stakes were planted in the ground. To each of them was lashed an Indian who had been burned to death.

Orellana's face became grim when he saw this evidence of Pizarro's revenge. He shook his head disapprovingly. "This is not the best way to march through a strange country," he said. "Let us be careful not to follow the example set by Captain Pizarro. He is a stern leader, and sometimes his unruly temper inclines him to do things that will merely enrage the tribes still more."

Living as best they could, Orellana's men struggled on through the forest. Sometimes they shot and ate a type of large tree lizard called an iguana. When they were very lucky they managed to kill a sloth, which is a kind of small tree bear.

These traveling conditions were too hard for the Indians from Guayaquil. They were men of the open plains and quite unaccustomed to the forest. A few of them had been killed in the fighting, but the others merely sickened and died. At night they would lie down beside the smoky fires, and in the morning they would be dead.

"Superstition is killing them," Orellana declared. "I remember how unwilling they were to sleep in that deserted Inca palace in the mountains. They said it was haunted by the spirits of dead emperors who had lived there. That was the night we had to drive them inside so that they would not die of cold. I heard them whispering that the royal curse would fall upon them and bring death. Believing such things, they are now very willing to die."

Whatever their illness, the wretched porters went on dying. On the day when all but two had gone, and the Spaniards were heavily burdened with the few supplies they could still carry, Orellana and his men came unexpectedly to Pizarro's camp.

In a swampy clearing beside some ruined native huts, gray canvas tents stood in untidy rows. Horses were tethered in the shade of trees, and pigs rooted noisily behind wooden rails. Yet to Orellana and his twenty-four men, the most welcome sight was the red-and-yellow flag of Spain flying over the pavilion where Gonzalo Pizarro would be awaiting them. It was the end of April, 1541. Six weeks had passed since Orellana, determined to keep his promise, had led his valiant men out of the mountain town of Quito. The whole journey had taken the lives of three hundred Indian porters and all but five horses.

Chapter Three

The Coming of the Canoes

GONZALO PIZARRO gave Orellana and his party a good-natured welcome. Being a well-bred Spanish gentleman, he pretended not to notice their rusty armor, their tattered and dirty clothing, or the lack of stores, left behind with the dead Indian porters. He ordered new tents to be erected, and made sure that the hungry men were given food as quickly as possible.

43

Orellana—who saw more with his one eye than most men see with two—quickly realized that things were not going well with Gonzalo's army. The handsome Pizarro was accustomed to the splendid battlefields of Europe, the sound of martial trumpets, the flutter of banners, and the silvery gleam of lance and sword. In the damp heat of the South American jungle there were none of these things. A high wall of greenery surrounded the clearing where the army had encamped. Monkeys and parrots screamed and jabbered incessantly in the trees. Rain fell daily in heavy showers, and the hot sunshine that followed caused steamy mists to rise from the ground. Even the best and strongest clothing rotted quickly in such a climate. Swords and armor had to be cleaned with oil and grit daily to avoid rust. When darkness came, myriads of fever mosquitoes swarmed from the wet undergrowth to cluster on the faces and arms of the weary men.

Gonzalo Pizarro hated the brooding forest around him. He loathed the discomfort of damp clothing and mildewed blankets. Being unable to speak a word of any native dialect, he mistrusted and despised all Indians, even the friendly ones who ventured near the camp.

All who showed any sign of hostility, he ordered to be hanged or burned.

"You have obtained, perhaps, some news of the cinnamon forests?" Orellana asked cautiously. He was sitting in Pizarro's tent and drinking a glass of sour wine, which was all his host could offer him.

Gonzalo shrugged his shoulders. He nodded impatiently toward the darkening jungle, where fireflies were already glimmering. "How does one find out anything in this forsaken country?" he demanded. "I had Indian guides who were either fools or rogues. Some deserted, others died. The two who still remain insist that we are near the place where the trees are said to grow, but how do I know if they are speaking the truth? And when we reached this miserable clearing, I had to rest our men awhile, for some are sick and others were wounded in our fights against the Indians who attacked us along the way."

"And of El Dorado himself?" Orellana asked.

Gonzalo shrugged. His good-looking face was sulky, and the heat of the night was making him sweat. "No news at all. Sometimes I wonder if the emperor really exists, or his country either, for that matter."

Orellana put down his empty glass. "If you will allow it, Captain Pizarro, I will speak with those two Indian guides of yours who are still alive. Perhaps they can tell me something useful."

Until late that night, Orellana squatted in a clumsy thatched hut that was lit by the flickering light of a rag floating in a saucer of palm-nut oil. Facing him were the two Indian guides. They were long-haired, silent fellows, with dark, slanted eyes, and bare bodies the color of worn copper. They talked in low, gruff sentences with long silences and slow, pointing movements.

Next morning, Orellana went to Pizarro's tent. "The cinnamon forest is at a place called Canelos," he said. "It lies far to the east of this place. The guides know nothing of El Dorado. One says the whole story is a lie. The other says there was such a ruler in the old days, but he has been dead a hundred years, and his kingdom is no more."

"What is the distance to Canelos?" asked Pizarro. "If we can but find that accursed forest, its spice will mean great wealth for us."

"The Indians say it will take seventy days to go there," Orellana replied. "They have not been to the place themselves, but they can ask the way from the tribes who live in the jungle."

Pizarro made an impatient gesture. "Seventy days in these accursed thickets, where a man cannot breathe properly, and must engulf flies with every mouthful of food he swallows! No matter; I will lead a party to Canelos tomorrow. You, Orellana, my loyal friend, will remain here to keep order in the camp. I regret that some of my men are beginning to grumble and show signs of mutiny. You may have to hang a few as an example to the rest."

Gonzalo Pizarro and seventy men disappeared into the dripping gloom of the rain-wet forest. Lean, polite Orellana took over command of the camp at Zumaco, which was the Indian name of the place.

His gaze was unusually severe, and his gentle voice very firm. "None of you shall strike or threaten an Indian," he said. "Understand, gentlemen, they are more numerous than ourselves, and can therefore be a dangerous enemy. Keep your weapons and armor clean; leave me to deal with the tribes."

Word passed mysteriously through the jungle that in the white men's camp there was now a one-eyed chieftain who spoke gently to all, and paid with beads and cloth and needles for any food brought to him. Shy and frightened Indians began to appear from among the trees. They brought live monkeys and river fish, bear meat and palm-leaf baskets filled with heavy-bodied eels. Gonzalo's men ate better than they had done since leaving Quito. To increase their rations still more, Orellana sent out parties to hunt across the open ground surrounding Zumaco. With crossbow and arquebus, the Spaniards succeeded in killing numbers of deer.

Orellana next turned his attention to the camp itself. "This place is unworthy of veteran soldiers like ourselves," he said. "We have brought spades with us. Let us see how working parties can improve our living quarters."

Sturdy little thatched huts began to replace the damp and leaking tents. Trenches were dug to carry away the rain water which sometimes flooded the whole camp. A big stone oven was built, in which Pizarro's Indian porters baked bread made with maize flour. A number of young pigs were killed and their flesh carefully cured.

While Orellana worked to preserve the health of the men and to better the conditions in which they lived, Pizarro and his seventy followers were groping through the jungle toward Canelos. It was the worst journey any of them had ever made. Their clothes were never dry, their stomachs never full. Indian villages became fewer, the jungle steadily thicker. But the day came at last when the Indians announced: "This is Canelos."

Pizarro peered around the dark and dripping forest. "Where?" he asked.

An Indian stepped up to a nearby bush and stripped off a piece of inner bark. "Eat," he said. "This is a cinnamon tree." The man was right; there was no mistaking the sweet, lingering taste.

"But where is the *forest* of cinnamon?" Pizarro demanded angrily. "All you do is point to one tree here and another yonder. They are too scattered through the jungle to be of any use to us."

The guide became sullen and afraid. "The Indians in the last village we passed said that this is the place named Canelos, and that it is here they get the spice which they carry to Quito. I know of no other place."

Gonzalo Pizarro, scowling with fury and disappointment, listened to the man's words but refused to be convinced. He had set his heart on making a great fortune from cinnamon, and he could not bear the disappointment of learning that he never would. He came of a family which was so noted for its cruelty in Peru that even some of the Spaniards—who were by no means sensitive in such matters—were shocked by the deeds the Pizarros often committed.

Gonzalo now seized captives from the nearest village and questioned them again through an interpreter. When the wretched Indians declared that they knew of no place where cinnamon trees grew more thickly, Pizarro ordered them to be tortured until they told what he said was the truth.

There was no such place. The Indians died miserably over slow fires, not knowing why they were being put to death.

Pizarro decided to continue marching eastward. He no longer knew what he was searching for, nor whither he was going. His temper grew worse and worse, and his followers began to grumble loud enough for him to hear.

"Must we wander forever in this wet quagmire?" they demanded angrily. "Is it right that we should go on eating parrots and monkeys and wild plums for the rest of our lives, or at least until our leader finds the kingdom of this dream king he calls 'El Dorado'? It would be better to return to Quito while we still have the strength to get there."

"They came out of the rain forests. Ahead of them stretched a level plain, covered with high green grass which reached to their knees. Once again they saw the blue sky overhead, and reveled in the heat of clear sunshine on their thin bodies and damp-rotted clothing.

"This is perhaps the border of El Dorado's country," said Gonzalo. "See how bright the sun is, and how refreshingly the wind blows. We will march on and see what we find."

He made camp and sent back an Indian messenger to Orellana. "Join me as quickly as possible," he wrote. "The guide will bring you to the place I have discovered."

Whatever Orellana thought of Pizarro's intention to plunge even deeper into the unknown heart of this country, he was loyal to his chief. Giving orders to the men to prepare themselves as quickly as possible for the march, he set about collecting all the provisions he could find for the journey.

When he joined Pizarro, the total force of Spaniards and their two hundred Indians tramped eastward across the breeze-swept prairie. They drove with them, as food, the sixty or seventy pigs still left alive.

The grassy plain came to an end after three days. Ahead of them the Spaniards saw with dismay the green barrier of the jungle which they had come to hate so bitterly. Now, also, there were rivers across their path: not wide and fierce and dangerous like those they had encountered on their march to Zumaco, but slow-rolling, muddy streams.

This was the end of August. After six months of marching and fighting, of constant damp and hunger and disease, the Spaniards had traveled only three hundred miles from Quito. By the end of the first three days in September, the forest was all around them again, the streams were merging into a leisurely river over a mile wide, and pigs were being eaten for lack of other food.

Deep-noted drums had sounded news through the jungle ahead of the tramping army. Bamboo huts in the little settlements were deserted; the fields were stripped of maize. Only a flashing spear or a yell of defiance from somewhere among the trees told the Spaniards they were being watched and followed all the time.

Even at this perilous stage of the journey, Pizarro would not treat any forest Indians they chanced to meet in a more gentle manner. He laughed when he saw Orellana busy practicing his dialects with the porters. "Why trouble your head with such labor?" Pizarro asked. "We still have sufficient guides from Quito to act as our interpreters. The language of our swords will serve better than words whenever these savages are in need of a lesson."

Pizarro and Orellana sometimes disagreed with one another more openly on the subject of Indians. They came to a village beside the river where the people were friendly. Their chieftain was a young, burly man with straight black hair. He was light-skinned—little darker than the sunburnt Spaniards, in fact—and his face was friendly.

"My name is Delicola," he said. "You are welcome here in our little village. We do not have great quantities of food, but we will do our best to feed you."

"We can trust him," said Orellana, who was watching Delicola's face. "At last we have found a friend on whom we can rely."

"We can trust no Indian," Pizarro answered sharply. "Like all his countrymen, this rogue will betray us whenever he gets a chance to do so."

There was nothing more that Orellana could do. Gonzalo Pizarro was the younger brother of the Viceroy of Peru, and the leader of the expedition. Orellana made a despairing gesture and walked away. Four days later, Pizarro had Delicola and three other chieftains bound with iron chains around their wrists.

"We will keep them as hostages," he said. "Should their people decide to attack us, they will lose their four leaders for good."

"I would have kept Delicola and his three companions as friends instead," said Orellana. "Then there would have been no need to keep them with us by means of an iron chain."

He went to comfort Delicola, who still remained friendly in spite of the humiliating treatment he had received.

"Our Captain is right," Orellana's twenty-four men from Guayaquil muttered among themselves. "There's hunger and death all around us. Delicola's tribe knows better than any Spaniard how to procure food in the forest. We remember how the Indians at Zumaco came from the jungle and brought us nourishment when they discovered that Orellana spoke their queer

tongue. Aye, Orellana is the man who knows best how to treat these odd people of the jungle."

For several days the Spaniards camped in Delicola's village beside the silent, greenish river. Pizarro studied his men and knew they would find it hard to march any further until they were rested properly. Their bearded faces were thin and a number of the Spaniards were suffering from fever or wounds that were slow to heal in this tropical climate. The leather of their shoes was greenish and rotten after long exposure to the damp. Musketeers were forced to dry out their gunpowder by the heat of a cooking fire. Finally, the horses were bony and in poor condition. There was not enough maize to feed them properly; and if they were left without Indian attendants at night, they were attacked by great ugly vampire bats, which came to suck their blood, thus weakening them still further.

A number of long, heavy Indian canoes rested on the mud beside the river. Each of these craft would carry six or seven men. Pizarro looked at the canoes for a while, and an idea entered his mind.

He turned to Cristobal de Funes, a lean, wiry

cavalier who was always willing to attempt anything dangerous. "Cristobal," said Pizarro, "take ten of these canoes and enough men to fill them. See that they are well armed and ready to fight as well as paddle. Go down this river until you reach some settlement where there is maize for ourselves and our horses. Bring back as much as you can carry. It is obvious that this river is a better road than any we could chop through the forest."

There were no eager volunteers to man the canoes. The Spaniards of those days were usually unhandy fellows in any kind of boat. They dreaded deep water, for few of them knew how to swim. In any case, swimming would have been almost impossible in the armor they wore all the time. They hung back and muttered among themselves until Cristobal angrily called out the names of those who must go with him.

At dawn next morning the Spaniards unwillingly launched the canoes and pushed out from the shore. Few of them had any idea how to use a paddle, and none had tried doing so in an Indian canoe. Singly and in pairs, the boats started wobbling down the jungle-fringed river.

Hostile Indians were waiting for them a mile farther downstream. They watched the awkward progress the Spaniards were making and noted the clumsy movements of their paddles. When a trumpet sounded a signal blast, the savages came flying out to meet the Spaniards, in canoes they had kept hidden under the overhanging trees. Wonderfully expert paddlers sent the craft skimming across the surface of the river. Other Indians stood erect in the bow and stern, holding stabbing spears in their uplifted hands.

An Indian canoe rammed broadside into one filled with Spaniards. The latter were thrown, struggling and shouting, into the water. The spears came lunging down at them. Nine Spaniards died miserably. A second canoe was overturned in the same way. This time five Spaniards were killed. Churning water with their paddles, muttering prayers and curses, the remaining Spaniards fled upstream. The Indians chased them almost to Delicola's village. By keeping close together, the frightened Spaniards were able to find shelter behind the fire of crossbows and arquebuses, which killed some of the pursuing Indians.

Pizarro had made a bad mistake in not allow-ing his men to practice in the canoes before going any distance from the camp. Fourteen men now lay dead in the river because of this mistake. Even now, however, he was too obstinate to admit that savages could fight better on water than soldiers from Spain could.

"We must learn how to handle these canoes more cleverly," he said to Cristobal de Funes. "Tomorrow all of you must start practicing up and down this stretch of river by the village. Your canoes will be protected by our fire from the bank if those villains downstream try to attack again."

The unhappy Spaniards spent two days paddling up and down a few hundred yards of water. By the end of that time they had learned how to balance the canoes and to alter course with their paddles.

"Now go and bring back that maize," Pizarro said on the third day. "Remember your fourteen dead companions. Make the Indians pay for the sad damage they did to you."

The little flotilla of canoes crept down the river, keeping close to each other. The Indians hovered beside them all the way. When the Spaniards landed and began stripping the first plantation they reached, the savages howled with fury. Sweeping inshore, they leaped out of their canoes and came racing up the grassy beach, raising their weapons as they ran.

The Spaniards faced the enemy without alarm. Now there was good firm ground under their feet instead of a wobbling, cramped canoe. Putting down the sacks which contained the maize, they drew their swords and leveled their pikes.

Once again the natives discovered that wooden spears and stone-headed clubs were almost useless weapons against Europeans wearing steel armor strong enough to resist everything except a close-range shot from an arquebus or an arrow from an English longbow. The Indians died in scores, and their bodies lay sprawled along the bank of the river. One Spaniard was killed by a throwing spear which struck him in the forehead, and a few of his companions suffered painful flesh wounds. Sweating and breathless, covered with dust and blood and river mud, they scrambled into their canoes and fled upstream to the village. It hurt their intense pride to realize that they were more like a pack of thieves caught robbing an orchard than experienced soldiers and gentlemen of Spain.

When they disembarked at the camp, they expressed their opinion loudly in mutinous voices. "Devil take these canoes!" they exclaimed. "Must we fight like savages against savages, and lose our lives for a few wretched sacks of corn? Another excursion or two like this, and our bones will rot in the stinking mud of this infernal river."

Pizarro saw that his men were nearing a state of rebellion against him. He stood scowling with rage as Indian porters took the corn away to the camp. Orellana, lean and silent as usual, came strolling toward the canoes and the angry men. He listened for a few moments and then began speaking to Pizarro. They talked for a long while. The Spaniards who were watching noticed that this time it was Orellana who did most of the speaking, while Pizarro stood and listened in silence.

That night, after the men had finished a wretched meal of dried horseflesh mixed with maize and plant roots, Pizarro spoke to them in the glowing firelight. Sentries patrolling to and fro in the darkness tried to hear what he was saying, above the noise of pigs and horses and the growling of bad-tempered dogs.

"Companions," said Pizarro. "I have discussed our present situation with others, and we have decided that Indian canoes are unworthy vessels for Spaniards. Yet we must go farther down this river to get food for the marches that will take us, I hope, to the kingdom of El Dorado, or at least to the conquest of some fertile country which will add to the greatness of Spain in the New World. How shall we proceed? you may ask. This is my answer. Here in this village we will build a ship, in which some of us may voyage down the river faster than we could march along the bank."

Chapter Four

The Coming of the San Pedro

FEW of the gentlemen in Pizarro's army knew any trade except that of fighting. They were men who preferred to leave more humble tasks to others, believing that tedious labor was unworthy of their noble ancestry. Luckily, there were also a number of pikemen and foot soldiers, who had once followed some useful occupation before coming to seek their fortunes in the New World.

Diego Bermudez, the brown-faced seaman who wore gold earrings, had learned his trade in heavy fishing boats which trawled their nets in wild Atlantic seas. Diego Mexia, a dark and surly fellow, had been heard boasting that he was as skilled a carpenter as any in Spain. Pedro de Porres, a quiet, civil man, had once been a blacksmith, and understood the heating, shaping, and tempering of iron. With him were two other blacksmiths, skilled in the art of making nails. Domiguez Miradero, an aristocratic young officer, announced that he had formerly sailed small boats for pleasure and knew something about cordage and the rigging of sails. Another pikeman, Sebastian de Fuenterrabia, was a friend of Diego Bermudez and, like him, a deepwater seaman.

"We have enough men to build a good craft," said Pizarro. "Diego Mexia, the carpenter, will show us how, and the skilled workers must assist him." He paused before adding lightly, "The rest of us, gentlemen, must learn to help in any way we can, and wherever Mexia can use us. I, myself, will gladly volunteer to saw wood and will doubtless earn a great many blisters in the process."

There was no shortage of timber. Within a

few hundred yards of the camp, there grew a sufficient variety of trees to make a dozen vessels of the type that Diego Mexia, the carpenter, designed. While axes swung and crosscut saws rasped back and forth, Pedro de Porres made charcoal for his little steel anvil, and the two blacksmiths started making six-inch iron spikes out of horseshoes. Panama and Number Five were handy fellows, who learned to use hammers, chisels, and long-handled adzes. Spanish aristocrats, who had never imagined themselves doing such work, carried lengths of timber on their shoulders, or learned how to guide a plane and hold a hammer correctly. Delicola and his three moody companions probably enjoyed seeing their captors toiling like slaves in the scorching heat. They came day after day to sit in a patch of shade under a tree and watch the vessel take shape.

The boatbuilding began at the end of September, 1541. Three hundred Spaniards worked with fearful haste and energy. They knew that starvation awaited them in a matter of weeks. The last of the pigs would soon be eaten, and after that there would only be a choice of horse or dog flesh. Killing off the horses might encourage lurking Indians to attack more fiercely.

The dogs served as valuable sentries during the night, for they growled whenever they scented a prowling Indian. Delicola's own people had flitted away into the forest as soon as they saw that their chieftain was a prisoner in the Spanish camp. By his own foolishness, Pizarro had thus destroyed the possible chance of obtaining food through the help of the Indians. In all that green twilight of forest, there was little to eat—or at least little that the Spaniards could recognize as food. They occasionally shot a monkey or a bird, but for the most part they were forced to depend entirely on their own dwindling stocks.

The vessel which Diego Mexia built was a heavy barge, about twenty-six feet long and nine feet wide. Its planking was an inch thick, and there were seats for ten rowers who would sit in pairs. The bow and stern were enclosed by a little deck, in which precious supplies of gunpowder, spare bowstrings, and food would be protected from sunshine and heavy rain.

When the hull of the vessel was finished, there remained the problem of waterproofing the seams between the clumsy planks. Mexia, who became gloomier and more quick-tempered every day, thought for a long while as he sat and gazed at these ugly seams. One day he went off into the jungle beside the village. He returned with a quantity of wild-growing cotton and a helmet full of resin, which he had collected from a tree.

"They'll serve better than nothing," he grumbled. "We will wedge the cotton between the planks and pour melted resin on top of it."

There were two priests among Pizarro's men. One of them, Father Carvajal, was a big, burly man. The other, Father Vera, was thin and somewhat given to complaining. On the day when Mexia announced that the boat was ready for launching, both priests spent the morning praying that the craft would float properly.

The Spaniards placed tree trunks on the ground to act as rollers. They fastened stout lianas to the bow of the boat and began to heave. Slowly, with much rumbling and creaking, the heavy craft slid down the bank and splashed into the water.

"I name thee *San Pedro!*" cried Pizarro, as the boat swung up and rested on the surface of the river.

"*San Pedro*," repeated the perspiring Spaniards. "May God grant that she bring us better fortune than we enjoy at present."

Diego Mexia stood on the shore and eyed the boat he had built. Perhaps to conceal his pride, or to hide his relief that she floated at all, he began to criticize. "A trifle broad in the beam," he muttered. "She floats a few inches too high for my liking. See how that wretched cotton and resin have not entirely prevented the seams from leaking. We must sink the boat with heavy stones until her timbers swell and tighten."

While the boat lay submerged beside the shore, Pizarro gave instructions as to how the march would continue. Twenty-one men would form a crew for the boat, which was to be fully laden with all the cargo she could carry. Another fifty Spaniards were to man the canoes. They would paddle close to the brigantine, as the *San Pedro* was called, if the Indians attacked the canoes. Crossbowmen and arquebusiers in the vessel would give covering fire. Pizarro and Orellana would follow the river's course on foot, accompanied by the rest of the Spaniards, the Indians, and the remaining horses. At nightfall, the *San Pedro* and the canoes would come ashore, to make camp with the party who were traveling by land.

The Spaniards' journey down the unknown

river began early in November, 1541. They named the camp they were leaving *El Barco,* meaning "the ship."

There was no protection from the sun for the Spaniards aboard the brigantine, nor for those huddled in the uncomfortable canoes. The heat made them weak and giddy. Swarms of insects tormented them all the while. Nevertheless, they were more fortunate than their companions ashore. The jungle became even denser. The ground was low-lying, and there were stagnant swamps where the river had flooded its banks during heavy rain. Great alligators swarmed and wriggled through these stretches of stinking water. Dangerous, bright-colored snakes slid through tangles of vegetation high above the floundering men. Unending attacks by mosquitoes caused the Spaniards' faces to swell until their eyes were merely narrow slits; and horrible brown leeches dropped from leaves and twigs to fasten themselves on faces, necks, and unprotected legs. Rotting trees underfoot sheltered centipedes as long and thick as a man's finger, and big black scorpions, whose poisoned bite was sufficient to cause the strongest man to groan in agony for hours.

Every once in a while, the marching Spaniards came to a small Indian settlement. The huts in these villages were made of woven reeds and roofed with grass. On an acre or two of roughly cleared land beside the huts grew white-flowered yucca plants, whose potato-like roots served as a starchy food. The Indians always fled before the Spaniards arrived and hid fearfully in the jungle. But after the first three weeks of their journey, the soldiers found fewer and fewer of these little settlements. The choking, dripping, and insect-haunted vault of jungle was too appalling for even river Indians to choose as a home.

The Spaniards in the *San Pedro* came to a place where another river joined their own. The united rivers grew mightier and their current rolled onward faster. Tiny islands covered with bright green grass and flower-bearing trees were dotted across the surface.

"Perhaps the growing size of the river is a good omen," the Spaniards suggested to one another. "Surely a mighty stream like this must support a native town somewhere along its banks? We may even be nearing the region where El Dorado—if such a man really exists—has his kingdom."

By the end of December, the Spaniards knew they were wrong. The forest was not thinning out, nor were there any signs of Indian villages. Swamps and deepwater creeks continued to bar the path of those who were traveling by land.

Perhaps the Indians who watched the building of the *San Pedro* knew what would happen to us, the Spaniards thought. They knew that we were going to die of hunger in these marshes.

Orellana was the only man who still remained friendly with Delicola. He also tried to obtain fresh information from the few Indian bearers who were still alive. "You will find no food in this region," said these men. "The Indians we met earlier told us that farther down this river there is a place where there are villages and wide plantations. We do not know if this story is true. Of one fact only are we sure. At the rate we are traveling daily, you will all certainly die of starvation long before you reach those villages. For ourselves we care not. Another day or two, and we shall be dead anyhow."

Orellana checked the truth of this story with the enchained Delicola. "It is true," said the chieftain. "For men such as yourselves, who know nothing of our river country, only death is waiting. A dozen times I could have shown you how to obtain food, but because of the unjust manner in which your leader, Pizarro, has treated me, I kept my lips closed. There *are* plantations downstream, but you will never reach them. Let me prove to you that at least part of what I say is true. You see those big green fruits on yonder shiny-leaved trees? Crush them and collect the juice. Then dam a stretch of this little stream beside us. Pour the juice into the water and you will see what happens."

Orellana collected a few of his men and did as Delicola suggested. The dripping, poisonous juice turned the water a pearly white. Quantities of dying fish rose to the surface almost at once, and the Spaniards collected them eagerly.

"Eat without fear," said Delicola. "Although these fish have died of poison, their flesh is not tainted in any way."

Orellana talked to Pizarro for a long time that evening while they sat eating the first fish they had tasted for weeks. "I do believe what Delicola says," Orellana declared. "Let him go with me in the brigantine, and I am sure he will lead us to the nearest plantations. We will gather as much food as we can carry and return here quickly."

"It is worth the effort," said Pizarro. "Take the sick with you in the boat, and some men who can row and fight. The rest of us will march on down the riverbank to meet you as you return."

"I may take Delicola and his friends?" Orellana asked again.

Pizarro shook his head. "No. Whatever you think of Delicola, my good Orellana, I trust him and his three companions only when they are chained together in a place where I can see them. They will continue to march with the rest of us."

Orellana studied Pizarro's obstinate face very carefully. It showed no sign of relenting. "Very well," he said quietly. "We will go without Delicola and his three friends. I will tell them what we intend to do."

Delicola sat looking at the ground while Orellana told him the decision. He made no sign of disappointment or anger. "I hope that the God you Spaniards worship will help you," he said. "I wish you good fortune, for you have shown nothing but kindness to my friends and myself in our present misfortune. Yet . . . I could have helped you on the river. It is no matter now. Good-by."

That evening, when the camp was asleep and only sentries watched drowsily in the darkness, Delicola and the three other chieftains walked silently out of the camp. They were still fastened together by the chain round their wrists. Not a dog barked, and no one saw them go. They vanished long before daylight and were never seen again. Perhaps they lived in that jungle and found a way back to their own country. Perhaps they died. Yet knowing the rain forests so thoroughly, and being accustomed to find food in places where others would starve, Delicola and the others might possibly have managed to survive.

Pizarro realized his mistake when he heard the news the next morning. He became silent and irritable. "Make haste and start the trip downstream," he said to Orellana. "Have the sick loaded into the *San Pedro* and take what other men you need."

Orellana chose all twenty-four of the men who had marched with him across the mountains from Guayaquil. He also took Panama and Number Five. Twelve sick men, among whom were Father Carvajal and Father Vera, were lifted into the boat. Twenty-one of Pizarro's men were also chosen. Among them were Diego Mexia, the boatbuilder, and Diego Bermudez, the seaman. A total of fifty-eight Spaniards and two Negroes settled themselves in the *San Pedro* and the canoes.

The boat lay deep in the water. Her cargo consisted of several hundred iron horseshoes, bolts of cloth, and waterproof Peruvian blankets made of llama wool. There were also supplies of tools, weapons, and gunpowder. Every man brought his own armor and a small bundle containing his personal possessions. Several leather sacks were filled with beads, mirrors, little copper bells, and knives, all of which would serve as presents for any friendly Indians they might encounter. With all this cargo aboard, it was no wonder that the twelve sick men had to rest on top of stacks of bales and baskets, where they were exposed to sun and rain.

The Spaniards who went with Orellana were a wild and strange-looking crowd. Their black beards and hair were long, matted, and carelessly clipped with daggers. The hot dampness of the river had yellowed their faces, and their cheeks were thin from hunger. Some were men who had fought in the conquest of Peru and

bore the scars of ancient wounds on their bodies. Three were over fifty years of age, but
they were hardy campaigners and wonderfully
skilled in the use of weapons. At least twelve
other Spaniards were not yet out of their twen-
ties. Red rust was forming on armor and weapons, and the padded cotton jackets, or *escaupiles*
(as they were called), were damp and moldy
and rotten. Indeed, Orellana and his followers
resembled a wild crew of river pirates, for there
was no knowing who among them owned great
estates in Peru, and who owned little except
the clothes they were wearing and the weapons
they fought with.

Such was the appearance of those fifty-eight
Spaniards and two Negroes when they began
their journey down the wide and breathlessly
hot river at the end of December, 1541. None
among them could have guessed that theirs was
the start of a voyage that would live forever as
one of the strangest adventures in history.

Chapter Five

A River Leads the Way

THE lofty and matted forest rose like high
green ramparts on either side of the river. The
trees were tall and thick-leaved and beautiful.
Lianas looped from their upper branches and
coiled from tree to tree. The warm air was
filled with the fragrance of flowers and the unceasing chatter of parrots and monkeys.

From bank to bank the river measured not

much more than a mile and a half in width, but it had become deeper and swifter during the past day or two. Orellana's men glanced overside at the bright, greenish water and wondered nervously whither the current might be taking them.

"This is the greatest river we have ever seen," they declared. "Only God can say when and where it comes to an end—perhaps in some vast cavern under a giant mountain, or in an unknown sea."

Orellana noticed his men's unhappy faces and fearful eyes. "Why trouble your heads about such unknown matters?" he asked. "Once we find yucca plantations, and perhaps a field or two of maize if we are lucky, we shall return upstream to meet Captain Pizarro and the rest of our companions. I do not think, *compañeros*, that this voyage of ours will be overlong. Once we have collected enough food, we will undoubtedly return westward to Quito and Guayaquil, leaving El Dorado to enjoy the pleasures of his golden kingdom for a while. Our only worry now is to secure food for our weary comrades on shore."

Diego Bermudez and Sebastian de Fuenterrabia, the deep-sea sailors, shared neither Orellana's optimism nor the fears of his men. They sat watching the distant shores. Sometimes they dropped a chip of wood overside and carefully watched the speed with which these fragments drifted astern. Every now and then they scratched a mark on the wood beside them with the point of a dagger.

When the sixty men camped ashore that night, Orellana glanced at Diego Bermudez in the firelight. "What is your reckoning of the distance we have come today?" he asked him.

"A little over seventy miles, Captain."

Sebastian de Fuenterrabia, a dark-eyed little man from Santander, on the coast of Spain, nodded agreement. "The river runs at three miles an hour," he said. "Our *San Pedro* has been traveling twice as fast for twelve hours. The figure I had in mind, Captain, was seventy-five miles."

Orellana said no more. He went on eating stewed monkey meat, to which Panama had added a few grains of maize and some wild onions. A new problem was arising in his mind.

Gonzalo Pizarro and those with him would be unable to cover more than seven or eight miles a day through the forest. Thus Orellana and his men were already sixty miles ahead of them, and there was still no sign of the yucca plantations which the Indians had said existed.

The second day was luckier for the crew of the *San Pedro*. One of the four arquebusiers on board managed to shoot a small alligator as it lay basking on the mudbank in midstream. That night the men roasted and ate its flesh. When the meal was ended, Orellana asked once again, "How far today?"

"Ninety miles, Captain," Diego Bermudez answered. "The river runs a little faster."

"A hundred," said Fuenterrabia. "Possibly my figure is a little high."

The third day of the voyage went by. There were still no signs of any plantations, nor did the Spaniards find any animal they could kill for food. That evening, the two sailors reckoned on a distance of ninety miles for the length of the day's voyage down the river.

Two more days went by. The *San Pedro* continued to creep down the river, which lay like a ribbon of silver between shores of emerald green. By the morning of the sixth day, the Spaniards were starving. They staggered down to the boat while the forest was asteam in the early rays of the sun, and dropped wearily into their places. The night before, they had

plucked a few green bananas, some bamboo roots, and green herbs. All these things they had mixed with a chopped-up snake and stewed in a cooking pot. It was not much of a meal for sixty men, but there was absolutely nothing left to eat in the *San Pedro's* lockers.

They rowed all that day without tasting a mouthful of food. Intense hunger prevented them from sleeping properly that night. The sick men were growing worse; two of them were delirious and believed they were back in a cool mountain village in Spain.

Breakfast on the seventh day consisted of a few grasshoppers mixed with grass and the parings from the kernel of a half-rotten coconut they had found floating in the water. Even now, however, the gallant Spaniards were unbeaten. With bleeding hands wrapped in cloths, they kept tugging away at the oars until sunset. The delirious men were singing wildly most of the time, and Father Vera, who had been sun-struck, was constantly mumbling prayers or chanting snatches of psalms. By evening, one of the twelve sick men was approaching death. It was certain that unless the other eleven invalids got some proper food before long, they, too, would die.

"Five hundred and fifty miles since we left Señor Pizarro," Bermudez told Orellana that night. "Our progress is being slowed because we no longer have the strength to pull manfully at our oars."

About eleven o'clock on the morning of the eighth day, the *San Pedro* rounded a wide bend in the river. Orellana, who held the long steering oar in the stern, rose unsteadily to his feet. "Look yonder," he said. "There is food for us if we have but the strength to take it."

The rowers paused to turn their heads. Even the sick men rose up from their resting places to stare along the river.

An Indian village stood on the bank. There were perhaps thirty thatched huts, and the ground beside them was green with the leaves of yucca and maize plantations. Smoke was rising from cooking fires, and a number of naked children were scampering away from the river, where they had been playing in the shallow water. A score of warriors, brandishing spears and clubs, were running down to the edge of the river to defend their village.

Orellana pressed on the steering oar and guided the *San Pedro* directly toward the settlement. The ponderous oars quickened their rhythm as the rowers made a last effort. The heavy bow thudded against the mud. Spaniards leaped overboard and started wading toward the grassy bank. They stumbled with weakness as they walked, and cried because they scarcely had the strength to raise their discolored swords or level their pikes. Their feverish eyes were fixed on the cooking pots ahead of them, for they could smell roasting meat.

The Indians had never seen such men before. Perhaps they thought these staggering, sun-blackened figures were evil spirits. They turned and fled after their women and children, who had already disappeared into the forest.

The Spaniards overturned the cooking pots on the ground. Urged by hunger, they scrabbled in the grass for shreds of meat and grains of smoking maize, which they rammed into their swollen mouths. Others, eating voraciously as they went, carried steel helmets of food to their helpless comrades in the brigantine. Men dashed into huts and brought out calabash gourds containing an oily kind of drink made from crushed and fermented bananas mixed with spice and water. They cooled their scorched mouths with this potent liquor and reached out again to a cooking pot.

Half an hour later, with stomachs swollen and painful from unaccustomed quantities of food, and heads giddy from great drafts of Indian wine, most of the Spaniards lay asleep in the deserted huts. Only Orellana and a few sentinels struggled to remain awake. Sprawled along a seat in the brigantine, his beard greasy and matted with food, a sharp-bladed ax lying handily beside him, surly Diego Mexia alone remained to guard the boat he had built.

The Indians reappeared before sunset. They crept timidly along the edge of the jungle, and paused in amazement when Orellana called to them kindly in their own language. Slowly they approached him, and stood gazing with amazement as one Spaniard after another staggered out of the shady huts, where they had slept the afternoon away.

Presently some of the Indians went back into the jungle. They returned, bringing with them an elderly little man whose gray hair reached to his bare brown shoulders. This was their chief, Aparia, and his village was named Imara.

Orellana treated the old man as if he were a Spanish nobleman. He apologized for the rough manner in which his men had stormed ashore and fed themselves. He assured him that no harm would come to his people. Finally, he gave Aparia a number of small presents, which delighted the chieftain.

"You will have food in plenty while you remain in my village," said Aparia. "Now that my people know you have no wish to kill them, they will return to their huts. The men will hunt daily, and the women will cook for you."

Fires began smoking again in the village at dawn. Spaniards wandered up and down the grassy riverbank, eating roast fish and tender slices of crocodile meat, sweet lettuce cut from the heart of a palm tree, and bread made of maize flour. Following Orellana's instructions, even the most impatient Spaniards spoke politely and behaved carefully to Aparia and all his tribe.

On the fourth day in the village, most of the Spaniards had begun to recover their health and strength. Orellana ordered the brigantine to be cleared of all supplies which might be left in Aparia's village. He intended to fill the boat with maize, cured meat, and other food supplies for Pizarro and his army.

The Spaniards were a valiant crowd of adventurers, as brave as any of their nation who explored the New World; but they thought only with horror and dread of the return voyage up that pitiless river. They were convinced they could never succeed in accomplishing it.

"We have come six hundred miles," they said. "The current helped us all the way. How long would it take us to return against that current? A month? Six weeks? Or even two months? Why, all the supplies we put in the boat would be consumed before we reached Captain Pizarro and his men. We will not return. We will *not* destroy our strength and throw away our lives trying to row against the current of this mighty river."

The men were talking mutinously. Orellana stood eyeing their angry faces. Perhaps in his heart he knew that a return voyage was almost impossible. Yet because of his loyalty to Pizarro, he was ready to attempt it if the men would go with him. But only a handful of Spaniards stood by him now. Nearly fifty others, including the two priests, were violently against the idea.

"If you will not row the *San Pedro* upstream, will you march up the bank until we reach Captain Pizarro's army?" Orellana asked.

The men muttered and shook their heads.

"What, leave our sick comrades here at the mercy of the Indians! How far could we travel overland in a day? Ten miles, perhaps. Even though Pizarro is advancing in this direction, our journey would take at least a month. Besides, we are few in numbers, and some hostile tribe would undoubtedly attack us on the way. No, Captain Orellana! Go downstream and we will be your men. But we will *not* accompany you in the madness of a return voyage upstream."

Orellana was beaten. There was no friendship in his face for any of those around him, but his coldest glance was directed at Pizarro's men, who had accompanied him in the *San Pedro*. They, at least, should have been willing to risk their lives for their leader.

"If any of us ever live to reach safety again, there will be talk of desertion," Orellana said. "Pizarro may believe that I left him in the jungle when his need was greatest. If you are agreed that you will not go back up the river, then set down your decision on paper and sign it. I am jealous of my honor. I will have no man in Spain point an accusing finger at me and say, 'There is Orellana, the man who left his friend, Gonzalo Pizarro, to starve in the jungle.' By the document you sign, all men may know what really happened in this village of Imara."

One after another, the Spaniards scrawled their names. Only eight of them stood back and shook their heads. Diego Mexia, tall, lanky, and scowling, was among them. These were the men who were prepared to attempt a return voyage.

Orellana read the document and placed it in the leather case where he kept all his papers. "Now," he said, "you are free to elect a new leader if you choose. You have gone against me in my wish to return upstream. If you think any man among you can lead you down the river more safely than I can, choose him now."

Not one of the Spaniards wanted any other leader but Orellana. He was the only one among them who spoke the Indian languages, and they trusted his cool head and wise brain. Without argument, they declared loudly that they would follow him faithfully, until death overtook them or safety was reached.

"Very well," said Orellana. "I shall remain in command of you, but this is my first order. We shall stay here for at least two months, if possible. Pizarro may decide to build other brigantines and follow us downstream. Perhaps he will overtake us here in Imara. While we are waiting to see if he arrives, we will spend our time making more nails from horseshoes. The *San Pedro* must be in sound condition if we are going to make a long voyage in her, for none of us can say where or how this river ends."

Four of the Spaniards died a week after reaching Imara. Sebastian de Fuenterrabia, the sailor, was one of them. The clash of steel hammers on the anvil ceased while Father Carvajal and Father Vera read the burial service, and the Indians gathered round the open graves to stare in amazement. Moodily, the Spaniards returned to their charcoal kiln and nail making.

There were foolish and greedy fellows among these Spaniards. They noticed that some of the Indians wore small and crudely made gold ornaments. One way or another, they contrived to obtain these small articles, although they were deadly afraid that Orellana might discover what they were doing. Probably they frightened the Indians into handing over their possessions by pointing a dagger at them.

The time came when Aparia, the kindly chieftain, smiled no more. At the end of January, 1542, less than a month after the Spaniards had come to the village, he disappeared into the jungle. The rest of the tribe went with him. The ashes of the cooking fires grew cold beside the huts, and there were no Indians to bring daily supplies of food. By this time, the plantations of maize and yucca had been almost completely stripped to provide for the guests. The Spaniards had no idea how to trap jungle animals for food, nor sufficient skill to supply themselves with fish from the rivers. Their weaker comrades began to grow worse when they were deprived of proper rations. Those who still remained in good health regarded the hot and unfriendly jungle around them with fresh alarm, or glanced longingly at the nearby water. That wide river, rolling onward through the forest, was an open road awaiting them. It was their only chance of escape from this village of Imara, where seven Spaniards now lay buried in the soil. They scarcely paused to remember what Aparia had told them when they first came to Imara: that although they would find many fertile countries farther down the river, those regions were inhabited by mighty and ferocious tribes. Perhaps those to be feared most of all, old Aparia had declared, were the women warriors of a fair-skinned queen named Conori.

The Spaniards had laughed scornfully at the idea of being in danger from a crowd of women. They were sure of only one thing: that to return up this enormous river would be a journey beyond their strength. They must continue down it and venture into the unknown, which they feared less than what they knew already.

"We have waited long enough for Pizarro," they told Orellana. "He has not come. Doubtless he has turned back toward Quito. Let us depart now before the accursed heat and vapor and misery of this deserted village kill all of us."

Orellana agreed. The remaining supplies of food were only sufficient for another few days. Diego Mexia reported that the *San Pedro* was in sound condition.

On the fourth of February, 1542, Orellana, with forty-eight armor-clad men, the two priests, and Panama and Number Five, climbed aboard the *San Pedro* and their canoes.

As the long, heavy oars began to creak back and forth in the thwarts, and the boat rounded a bend in the river, the Spaniards saw Orellana look gloomily upstream. There was still no sign of Pizarro, and now the two parties could never hope to meet again.

Chapter Six

Fair Wind and Fine Weather

THE little *San Pedro* glided onward down the river. The air was cooler on the water, for the gentle breeze which came at dawn lingered until the white glare of the sun reached its greatest intensity in the middle of the day.

In the topmost branches of the forest, troops of monkeys clustered to stare at the distant boat. Their screaming cries disturbed bright-feathered parrots, which fluttered upward,

squawking, from the interlocked mass of leaves
and branches and coiling lianas.

When the sun was sinking behind the western fringe of the jungle, Orellana guided his
little fleet toward the shore. He would not take
the risk of continuing the voyage at night. No
man could guess what lay ahead of them. They
were terrified of being caught in monstrous
rapids, or being swept over a thunderous water-
fall when darkness surrounded them.

On the third day, a new tributary came
sweeping in to join the river from the north.
Blending waters boiled and surged and rum-
bled around the *San Pedro*, causing the vessel
and canoes to pitch and lurch alarmingly. Soon
the Spaniards realized that they were moving
downstream slightly faster than before. The
reinforced current was taking them along at
about four miles an hour, without the help of
oars. They looked at one another with relieved
faces as the frightening eddies were left behind.
Father Carvajal ceased muttering prayers under his breath.

There were no Indian settlements to break
the green monotony of the jungle. The Spaniards were forced to rely on the supplies of food
which still remained in the boat. But they were

becoming more skilled in the ways of the forest. Dominguez Miradero, the young nobleman who had sailed small boats for pleasure, had taken a couple of Indian fishing nets from Imara. It was clumsy gear, made of interwoven palm-leaf fronds, and only suitable for fishing in small creeks. Yet the nets served well enough. The Spaniards made a strange sight as they floundered back and forth in mud and water, seeking to grab little fish with their hands or to scoop them up in their helmets.

Panama and Number Five were developing an almost uncanny sense of knowing where to look for edible plants. They slipped away into the jungle whenever the *San Pedro* reached shore, and came back with tender roots, juicy leaves, and waxy berries, all of which could be eaten without harm.

Meanwhile the four arquebusiers and five crossbowmen in the company were constantly watching for the chance of a shot. Sometimes they managed to bring down a toucan or a heron, and every now and then they managed, with much rejoicing, to shoot a tapir—which is a piglike animal with a curiously long nose.

As the *San Pedro* lumbered on down the river, the Spaniards noticed that the weather was changing. "We're leaving the region of un-ending rain behind," they said. "For a whole day and a night now, not a drop has fallen. Also, the steam that rises from the jungle with the morning sun is growing thinner daily."

They relaxed and grew confident. Only Diego Bermudez, the sailor with the gold ear-rings, kept hourly watch on the sky while the *San Pedro* was in midstream. Since the death of Fuenterrabia, Diego was the only expert sea-man left in the expedition.

On the eighth day after leaving Imara, he called sharply to Orellana. "Captain, we must head quickly for the shore. Look at yonder clouds, I pray you."

From under the rusty brims of their helmets, the Spaniards stared up in sudden alarm at the western sky. A great mass of copper-colored clouds was rising above the endless rim of for-est, and quick stabs of blue forked lightning were flashing from one dark mass to another. The breeze had dropped. Above it rose a curi-ous, faint, humming noise, like that of a distant wire plucked taut. It filled all the air and kept growing louder.

Orellana nodded. "Aye," he said. "The sooner the better."

Diego tugged at the shaft of the steering oar. The boat started making for the fringe of greenery which marked the southern bank. The rowers swung back and forth on their thwarts energetically, and the canoes drew closer to the *San Pedro*.

The big boat crashed in among the undergrowth as the first gust of the approaching storm roared down the river. The surface of the water seemed to lift with the fury of the wind. The folded sail was ripped out of the *San Pedro* and went whirling aloft. Monkeys were torn loose from trees and hurtled, screaming with terror, through the air. The wind capsized a canoe, and the men struggled ashore through muddy water. Those aboard the *San Pedro* leaped overside and tugged with frantic strength, trying to run it onto a shelving bank of mud. The water rose round their ankles, then to their knees. It carried the brigantine deeper into the fringe of jungle.

The wind rose swiftly to a screaming, continuous blast. Whole trees were ripped clear of the ground and crashed into the river. The Spaniards found it impossible to remain erect against the frightful storm. They threw themselves face downward in the mud, where the tepid water of the rising waves washed against their bodies. The lightning grew brighter and fiercer. From the jungle came sharp, cracking explosions as tree after tree was struck by blue shafts of fire. Behind the wind and the blazing lightning, a wild torrent of rain came roaring through the jungle, flattening the foliage and creating such an uproar that speech was utterly impossible.

The fury of the storm lasted an hour. At the end of that time, the Spaniards lifted pale, mud-streaked faces to stare at a brightening sky. The thunder clouds were rolling on down the river; the roar of the tempest was fading away. Far to the west, sunshine was returning; and clouds of steam were already rolling upward from the saturated forest.

Down the river came floating the wreckage of the storm. Whole trees bobbed along with the current, turning over and over as they came. The surface was covered with a floating carpet of dead leaves, broken branches, and uprooted plants. Birds and monkeys came with this flotsam, and the few survivors among them sat precariously on tree trunks and stared about with frightened eyes.

The *San Pedro* was pushed back into the

river. Men climbed aboard her and unshipped their oars. Boat and canoes went on down the stream, borne faster than usual by the swift current of the flood. That evening, instead of camping on shore, they fastened their craft to an enormous tree which was floating in midstream. They built fires on the vast trunk, and ate a supper of monkey meat, roast heron, and bananas in a pleasant shelter formed by the leaf-covered branches, which rose high in the air around them.

When the men lay around their fires that evening, and starlight glittered on the dark water, Orellana had something to say. *"Compañeros,* in today's storm some of you were nearly drowned when a canoe overturned. It seems we will never be safe as long as we continue to use these canoes. They can be separated too easily from the *San Pedro* if Indians attack us before we can reach the shore. Therefore, we must build a second boat as soon as possible, and abandon our wretched canoes for good. . . . No, *amigos,* it is useless to grumble and mutter. As long as I remain your leader, it is my duty to do everything possible to safeguard your lives. If you think for a moment, you will realize that there is greater safety in a heavy boat than in a frail canoe. We will build a second boat as soon as we find a suitable place for the task."

Ten days after leaving Imara, the *San Pedro* came to a place where two more tributaries flowed into the main river. From bank to bank, the width of the stream was now four miles. The daily breeze blew a little more strongly, and the nights were a trifle cooler. Although maddening swarms of mosquitoes and other insects still haunted the jungles alongside the river, the Spaniards were almost free of such pests out on the wide surface of the stream. When the sail was drawing strongly and it was possible to ship their oars, they were able to rest and sleep. But the unfortunate men in the canoes had to keep on swinging their paddles from morning to night, exposed all the time to the cruel heat of the sun. They began to think better of Orellana's idea for a new boat.

"At least when it is built we will no longer have to toil like slaves," they said. "See how our comrades can repose at their ease in the *San Pedro* while we unlucky fellows must paddle for dear life to keep up with them."

For three weeks there was no sign of an Indian settlement, nor even a single hut. The end of February had almost come before the Spaniards saw another village, standing on the northern shore of the river. It was only a small place, holding not more than forty huts. These dwelling places had walls made of reeds plastered over with mud. Their roofs were thatched with a thick layer of brownish coconut fronds.

Ten miles farther downstream, a second village came into sight, then a third and a fourth. Each was bigger than the last, and the houses grew larger and more prosperous in appearance. Some had brown mud-brick walls and silvery-gray roofs and were surrounded by red-flowered hibiscus bushes. Around these villages were cool green plantations, where maize and yucca flourished in rich black soil reclaimed from the surrounding jungle. Down at the river's edge lay big canoes. Projecting above the water was the top of a closely built wooden frame, in which live turtles were imprisoned.

All the people in the villages stood on the bank to gaze wonderingly at the oncoming *San Pedro*. They were well-built people with dark-brown skins, naked except for a loincloth. Both men and women wore clumsy ornaments of wood and gold and feathers, and necklaces made from the vertebrae of snakes. The men

wore their hair at shoulder length, but the hair of the women was very much longer, black and wonderfully luxuriant.

Orellana examined the village attentively. "Steer for the shore," he said. "I think we have come to the place we are searching for."

Several hundred warriors crowded together when they saw the boats heading toward them. Clutching bows and javelins, they gaped and chattered when Orellana began leading his men ashore. The Spaniards wore mail and were fully armed. Their black hair and beards were long and matted, and the sun had reddened their skins. Weeks and months of travel had frayed the cotton shirts and doublets they wore, and rotted their leather shoes. Some of them were even barefooted, or wore sandals of pigskin they had cured and sewed for themselves.

The Indians decided not to fight. They lowered their weapons and began to smile and nod. Presently the bravest of them stepped forward and touched the Spaniards' bodies and weapons. Out of their midst came a middle-aged man with a broad and grinning face. "The drums told us there is one among you who speaks our language," he said. "Who is he?"

"It is I," Orellana replied. "Tell your men

to lay aside their weapons, O chief. We come not as enemies, but as weary travelers in need of food and rest."

The chief nodded. "Yes, we know you have come far down the river. My name is Aparia, the same as he who rules the village of Imara, where you stayed for a while. You caused no great harm to the people of Imara, so you are welcome in this village. Come. I will take you to huts where you and your friends may eat and sleep."

All that day, the Spaniards feasted or slept, drank sweet Indian beer, and rested in their cool huts. Whenever they appeared in the open, wondering crowds of people followed them, to offer gifts of fruit and fish and meat.

"How much farther does this river go?" Orellana asked Aparia, when the friendly chieftain came to sit by his fireside that night.

Aparia made a puzzled gesture with his hands. "Who can say, for none of us have ever voyaged to the end of it. Understand, white stranger, that farther down this river are many fierce tribes who would kill us if we tried to pass through their country. They are called the Machiparo. No doubt they will also kill you and your friends. Even if they fail to do so, it is certain that the women warriors of Queen Conori will leave none of you alive. I have heard that they dwell in a country not far from the place where the water becomes a river without banks."

A river without banks, Orellana thought to himself. He turned to Diego Bermudez and translated Aparia's remark.

"Aye, Captain," the sturdy Bermudez replied. "I have no doubt he means the sea. Ever since we embarked on this river we have come due east. If it continues to run the same way, we must reach the Atlantic Ocean sooner or later. I recall that some forty-two years ago, a navigator named Amerigo Vespucci, who came from the Italian city of Florence, sailed southward past the island of Trinidad until he came to the mouth of the greatest river he or any other man had ever seen. It flowed into the sea from a wild country of forest and jungle. I have an idea, but who knows for sure, my Captain, that we are embarked on that same river now."

Orellana looked shrewdly at Bermudez. "Yes, *amigo*, you talk good sense. I have already had the same idea. Our countrymen have not yet settled Trinidad, because of the great ferocity of the Carib tribes who live there. But west of Trinidad is the little island of Cuagua, which some call the Island of Pearls. A Spanish colony is located there to obtain the wealth of the sea. To reach them, we must sail northward, if God spares our lives until we reach the mouth of this river. And I pray this may be the river Captain Vespucci discovered so long ago."

Orellana glanced at Aparia. "Give us leave to remain in your village for a while, O Aparia, and you will see us build a vessel even larger than the one in which we came. We will cause you no trouble, and there will be presents for you and your friends when our task is done."

Aparia nodded. A smile appeared on his face. "When you were approaching my country," he said, "we discussed whether it would be better to kill all of you, or treat you as friends. I am glad we chose to make peace with you, for I see now that you are brave and clever men. Remain without fear and build your vessel. I am curious in my mind to learn how such work can be done."

Chapter Seven

The Building of the Victoria

THE open fields around the Indian settlement echoed with the clatter of hammers and the continual rasping of saws. Once again, Diego Mexia was in charge of the work, and every Spaniard was helping him. A Spanish aristocrat, with a ranch and slaves in Peru, pulled one end of a crosscut saw, while a humble fellow who owned nothing in the world except a few stolen gold brooches pulled the other end.

Alonso de Cabrera, a young gentleman of excellent family, was put to work trimming off the branches of a felled tree with an ax. Benito de Aguilar, who owned two thousand good acres near the city of Lima in Peru, found himself sharpening iron nails with a file. Lorenzo Munoz, a lanky fellow who was handy with tools but could neither read nor write, taught Aguilar how to do the job. Powerful Number Five helped his white masters carry the heaviest balks of timber from the jungle. Little Panama was busy supervising the Indian women who cooked meals for the Spaniards, and taking care of Orellana's needs. Father Carvajal and Father Vera were excused from heavy work but kept themselves busy picking wild cotton and collecting resin. Every morning and night the two priests held a religious service beneath the high wooden cross which Orellana had erected in the village.

Because they were always tired, the Spaniards had neither the time nor the desire to admire the beauty of the forest around them. High, graceful coconut palms flourished in groves close to the village. Banana plants, with monstrous leaves eight feet long and over a foot wide, grew in the shade of mighty flowering trees. Enormous clusters of yellowing fruit dangled from them. Giant blue, red, and yellow butterflies, with wings a foot in diameter, fluttered in the bright sunshine. In front of the peaceful village, the sparkling river went on flowing eastward at its same leisurely pace.

The end of March, 1542, arrived. Mexia had laid the keel of the new boat, and its ribs were being nailed into position. During that month, Juan de Alcantara, a young foot soldier, died of heatstroke. Some of his companions declared that vampire bats had emptied the poor fellow's veins of blood, because he could not tolerate the stuffy cotton cloths in which all the other men wrapped themselves at night for protection against the horrid brutes.

By the end of the second week in April, the new brigantine's planks were being fastened to the ribs with the long black nails which Pedro de Porres had made so cleverly on his anvil. The rest of the men were boiling resin to calk the seams, making eighteen-foot oars, or smoke-curing quantities of meat, which the Indians obtained from tapirs and a large river animal known as a dugong.

The second brigantine was built at last. Watching Indians screamed and pranced with excitement as the vessel went rumbling down the tree trunks and splashed into the river. Old Aparia shook his head and grunted in wonderment. He sat on the bank for the rest of the day, staring at the largest boat any of his tribe had ever seen.

The new craft was named the *Victoria*. Her length was thirty feet and her width ten feet. During the voyage down the river from El Barco, the *San Pedro* had occasionally suffered damage from collision with floating timber. Mexia gave the *Victoria* heavier planking, which was three inches thick. This made her somewhat ponderous; but because her design was better, it seemed likely that her speed would equal that of the *San Pedro*.

The Indians helped the Spaniards to load both vessels for the trip. Enough provisions were stowed on board to last Orellana and his fifty-one men for ten days, if they were careful. Orellana chose to go in command of the *Victoria*. He put a hardheaded and tough old veteran named Cristobal de Segovia in command of the *San Pedro*. The Spaniards who had wearily paddled the canoes for the amazing distance of more than a thousand miles found places for themselves in the brigantines, and glanced thankfully at the tapering masts above their heads.

Aparia came down to the water's edge to see the brigantines depart. "I do not think you will ever reach the River-Without-Banks," he said to Orellana. "Your enemies will overwhelm you like the dreaded shoals of little piranha fish, which attack any living animal. But I think you will succeed in going farther than any of my tribe could manage to go. Good-by. May the gods of our forest go with you."

The *Victoria* and the *San Pedro* were steered into midstream. The current began to carry them forward. The Spaniards had a final glimpse of kind old Aparia, standing beside the river and examining with speechless delight the fine steel sword Orellana had given him. Beside him, other Indians were exulting over beads, knives, and bells. Their cries of delight and gratitude came faintly across the water.

Orellana and his men had spent two months in Aparia's friendly village. This was their longest stay anywhere during the voyage down the river.

The brigantines reached the frontiers of the

Machiparo's region about ten days later. By that time they had gone seven or eight hundred miles farther downstream. An apparently unending village of dome-shaped grassy huts stretched along the northern bank of the river. Neighboring plantations were divided into plots, and neat wooden fences stood around some of the larger houses. Here and there were vast flattened squares of beaten earth, surrounded by level grassy banks, which appeared to be meeting places for the Machiparo people.

The warriors of this tribe gave Orellana no chance to call a peaceful greeting to them. When the brigantines were almost opposite the village, hundreds of warriors rushed to the edge of the river. One after another, forty-foot canoes started darting out from the shore. Each vessel was paddled by twelve or fourteen men seated at bow or stern. Amidships sat thirty naked fighting men, their faces and bodies smeared with vivid stripes of ocher. They were holding broad-headed throwing spears and enormous shields made of water-hardened leather.

"We must keep close together," Orellana said. "If either boat gets surrounded, its crew may be overwhelmed."

The Spaniards stopped rowing to put on their steel corselets and helmets, which the heat of the sun had made them lay aside. Arquebusiers kindled the slow-burning lengths of fuse with which they kindled the powder in their weapons. Crossbowmen hauled steel springs and slid heavy bolts into the grooves. Father Carvajal and Father Vera, a most fearless pair, stood upright and began praying aloud for victory in the approaching fight.

The sound of their calm voices was lost in the wild shouting of the Indians aboard the canoes. The Machiparoans were absolutely fearless. Singing wild, barbaric chants, they came straight at the brigantines. So fast did their canoes travel under the thrust of paddles swinging in perfect unison, that a bow wave curled outward from each one.

As they neared the brigantines, warriors rose up to hurl spears from a short wooden rest, which gave the hurtling weapons tremendous speed and force.

The Spanish crossbowmen and arquebusiers began returning the fire, but there were a mere nine of them altogether. They could get away only one shot a minute, and perhaps less, with their clumsy weapons. A canoe came flying in toward the *San Pedro*. Its bow crashed against the brigantine's side. As the yelling savages leaped aboard, they were met with swinging swords and darting steel lances. One after the other, they fell backward into the water. After that, the rest of the canoes circled the brigantines at a range of thirty yards and kept up a tremendous shower of javelins.

"Make for the shore," said Orellana. "We must show these people that we intend to go on down the river and that they cannot stop us. If they will not barter with us for food, we must take it."

The brigantines ran aground on a shelving bank below the village. The Spaniards waded ashore, formed themselves into two ranks, and began to advance up the slope. Ten of them stayed behind to guard the boats, assisted by Panama and Number Five. The Negroes were gray with terror, but they valiantly grasped steel-headed pikes and stood ready to fight beside their masters.

A roaring mass of several hundred Indians came rushing down the grassy incline to meet the oncoming Spaniards. With spear and club they leaped at their mailclad enemy.

The Spaniards reeled back under the shock

of the collision, but they soon rallied. They were expert fighters with sword and pike and ax. Slowly they began to advance again, driving the Indians before them. Spears thudded harmlessly against protecting mail. Mighty blows from descending war clubs dented Spanish helmets and sometimes half stunned the wearers, but not one of Orellana's men fell dead. They feared only for their legs, which, from knee to ankle, they had left unprotected by armor, carelessly believing the Indians would not fight with any valor on land. Had the Machiparoans taken the opportunity to aim low with their spears, probably none of the Spaniards would have survived. Yet for some strange reason, which Father Carvajal afterward declared was due to God's mercy, the Indians thought merely of striking their enemy on the head or the body. No doubt it was the only kind of warfare they had ever known.

Another wave of Machiparoans charged down the river toward the brigantines. Father Carvajal and Father Vera promptly retreated to the stern to be out of the way.

The ten Spaniards left to guard the boats were almost rolled underfoot in the surging onslaught. They slashed and stabbed with frantic speed as the Machiparoans poured over the thwarts in an unending brown wave. The giant Number Five, normally a peaceful fellow, seized a pike and killed one attacker after another. Neither he nor his friend Panama wore armor of any kind, yet they fought fearlessly beside the Spaniards, while the priests shouted encouragement or else beseeched Heaven to bring confusion to the enemy.

Breathless, bruised, and shaken, those Spaniards who had followed Orellana ashore struggled into the village. Some of them seized bags of maize, live turtles, cured meat, or any other provisions they could see. Others held off the howling mass of Machiparoans, who were still fighting with unabated fury. Their numbers and the ferocity of their attack steadily increased. The Spaniards found themselves unable to swing their swords in the narrow space between the huts. Machiparoans swarmed across the roofs and stabbed downward with their lances, or hurled lumps of rocks onto the heads of their enemies below. By this time more than two thousand Indians were attacking the Spaniards, who had been fighting without pause for two hours.

"Get back to the boats," Orellana shouted.

"Those carrying provisions will go first. The rest of us will fight a rear-guard action."

The Spaniards began to retreat toward the river. On seeing this, the Indians reorganized themselves and charged again. Five of the weary Spaniards were knocked down by war clubs and had to be helped to their feet. Another ten were wounded by thrusting spears.

Streaming with perspiration and smeared with blood, the Spaniards at last reached the brigantines and dropped their loot aboard the vessels. By this time some of them were so weak from wounds, or so dazed by repeated blows, that their comrades had to carry them part of the way.

Those who were strongest settled themselves at the thwarts and unshipped the heavy oars. Others waded knee-deep in the water and thrust the boats clear of the bank. The rest beat off the hordes of Indians who came charging with unquenched fury into the deepening river to hurl one last dart or deliver one final blow.

The Spaniards rowed hastily into midstream and left their enemies behind them. The noonday heat of the sun was scorching, and there was no breeze for the sails. The brigantines crawled along, while the men toiled to clear up the litter of broken spears and lances, wash the planking clean of blood, and attend to twenty wounded comrades. They were silent as they worked, and a little afraid. Although they were veteran fighters, the ferocity of the Machiparoans was worse than anything they had ever seen in Peru. Such attacks could not be beaten off many more times. They ransacked the baggage for lengths of armor called greaves, which would protect their lower legs, and for mailed gloves and face guards. Earnestly they prayed that the Machiparoans would leave them alone after this one battle.

The Indians had no intention of doing so. All that night they came charging out of the darkness in their canoes, to hurl javelins and slingstones at the boats. The weary and haggard Spaniards found little chance to rest and no chance at all to sleep. They went on rowing and fighting all that night, while the river around them echoed with the savage war cries of their enemies.

Orellana ordered the *San Pedro* and the *Victoria* to steer for a sandy islet in midstream which had become visible at dawn. Some of the wounded were in a bad way; their injuries needed careful attention, which it was impossible to give them in the boats.

"These devils are more expert on water than we are," Orellana said. "Perhaps they will hesitate to attack on land, where one of us is worth thirty of them."

The islet was not more than three hundred yards wide and about four hundred yards long. Along its center grew a fringe of palm trees and a natural wall of shrubs and tall grass. The Spaniards staggered ashore, aching from their bruises and wounds, and lay down on the warm ground to rest. The Machiparoans paddled around to the far side of the island, crept inland, and burst through the mesh of undergrowth in a roaring and bloodthirsty horde.

The Spaniards were driven back into their boats. Some of the Machiparoans actually leaped aboard the brigantines after them, stabbing and slashing at them. These Indians were killed and their bodies thrown over the side, but they succeeded in wounding several more Spaniards, some of whom were already suffering from three or four injuries.

On down the river went the little *San Pedro* and the *Victoria*. After them swept a fleet of big canoes, with drums pounding, wooden trumpets blowing loudly, and savages yelling in fierce excitement.

The crossbowmen and arquebusiers did everything they could to hold the canoes at bay. It was clear that the Machiparoans feared the flash and roar of the clumsy guns, each loaded with two or three bullets, more than they did the silent yet deadly crossbows. Each time one of the arquebusiers aimed at a canoe, the crew paddled hastily out of range. There came a nervous few moments for Orellana when raindrops spattered down from a passing cloud. The Spaniards glanced up at the sky and prayed that no heavy rain would come. A downpour would wet the gunpowder and ruin the crossbow strings. If these weapons became useless, the Indians would almost certainly overwhelm the boats.

The villages of the Machiparo stretched along the bank of the river for mile after mile. The Spaniards had reached the first one about the fifth of May, or some ten days after they had left their peaceful camp in Aparia's settlement. They did not see the last of the hostile villages until the tenth of May, by which time they had rowed and fought their way down three hundred miles of river.

At dawn on the eleventh of May, they saw untouched jungle growing down to the edge of the river, and no sign of another enemy village ahead. Far astern, the last of the pursuing canoes were returning up the river, and the noise of pounding drums was growing faint.

"Rest while you can," Orellana said to the hungry and exhausted crews. "Aparia told me that beyond the country of the Machiparo lies that of the Omagua, another violent tribe. These warriors will be at us as soon as we reach their territory. We may have perhaps two days of peace, *compañeros,* before we fight again."

All that morning, the boats drifted with the current, while the utterly weary men sprawled asleep on the seats or lay groaning with the pain of their wounds. At noon, when the sun was directly overhead and the woodwork too hot to touch, the Spaniards rowed to the southern bank. The width of the river now lay between them and any lurking Machiparoan canoes. They limped ashore, built fires to cook food for themselves, and dropped to the ground to rest. Every hour the patrolling sentries wakened others to take their places, and then sank down in weary sleep.

Late in the afternoon, the Spaniards awak-

ened and began to think hungrily of food. "There's little enough for us," said Orellana. "The supplies we took from the village are almost finished. Let the crossbowmen and arquebusiers see what they can do to provide us with an evening meal."

The famished men went roving through the woods. Some killed snakes with their swords. Others managed to net a few small fish in a nearby shallow creek. One party chased and wounded a small alligator, but the brute escaped from them among the tangled roots of mangrove trees in a deep and muddy pond. For dinner that night, the fifty-two men ate a peculiar concoction they had stewed in their iron cooking pots. Two herons, several snakes, a number of fish, three monkeys, and a couple of handfuls of dried maize were the principal items. Yet so accustomed were the men to hardship by this time, that they were able to joke about this meal.

"I have eaten tender Castilian lamb broiled in red wine over a charcoal fire," said Alonso de Cabrera, the young aristocrat. "I do not recall that it tasted sweeter or more tender than this excellent stew with which I have filled my stomach tonight. Given a little salt, which regrettably we lack, I declare that even our King —God bless him—might enjoy such an excellent meal!"

They slept ashore that night in the hot silence of the jungle. A fresh breeze came at midnight, and Diego Bermudez awakened to sniff it. "It blows from the east," he murmured. "This is something new. Until now it has nearly always come from the west."

At daybreak they ate what was left of the stew and launched the boats again. That day, a middle-aged cavalier named Mateo de Rebolloso died of wounds. He was buried ashore, and the voyage went on. Late in the afternoon, they came to the first of the Omagua villages. It was a dark, dirty place of low huts and muddy paths, surrounded by a high palisade of wooden stakes. The yucca plantations were badly kept and overgrown with weeds. The warriors who lived here were different from the Machiparoans, short, dark-skinned, and ugly. Most of them had pierced noses, and they wore bright feathers or colored wooden plugs in the holes. Yelling, and shaking their spears, they rushed down to the edge of the river but went no farther. Unlike the Machiparoans, they did not try to attack in canoes.

Grim and red-eyed, Orellana stood up in the *Victoria* to speak to them. He had slept little during the past week, for he had spent many of the nights caring for the wounded. His usual good temper and patience were beginning to wane. "Put aside your weapons," he called. "We will take nothing from you except in exchange for the presents we can give you."

The Omaguans screamed a derisive answer. They hurled their javelins upward in a curving arc, so that the hurtling weapons fell into the boats.

Orellana stooped and picked up his sword. "Since that is their answer," he said, "we must fight. That village yonder means rest for our wounded companions and food for us all. Come, *compañeros*, let us fight for a night's shelter under a roof and the comfort of a well-fed stomach."

Forty-seven Spaniards splashed through the shallow water to follow their leader ashore. They were grim and angry men, determined to kill anyone who tried to hold them back from the village. With sword and crossbow, ax, pike, and arquebus, they smashed through the ranks of the Omaguans. A couple of hundred Indians died in that brief but ugly fight beside the river.

The rest of them ran into the forest, where the women and children had already taken shelter.

That night the Spaniards ate roasted yucca and smoke-dried turtle meat. They ended their meal by drinking sweet banana wine from a great vessel made out of the hollow butt of a palm tree.

"This liquor has not the mellow flavor nor the purity of our own good Spanish wine," they declared. "Yet under its livening influence, a man may forget his miseries of today and dream only of the good fortune he will enjoy tomorrow."

Chapter Eight

The Coast of Enemies

WHILE the Spaniards were resting for nearly a week in the captured village, they argued among themselves about how far they had traveled since first taking to the river. Some said the distance was nearly three thousand miles, others said it was less than that. A few humorous ones, glancing at their ragged clothes and rust-stained weapons, declared that they had been traveling so long that they had forgotten in what *year* they had begun the voyage, and therefore could not be expected to remember smaller details such as miles!

Diego Bermudez, the seaman, and Cristobal de Segovia, the middle-aged, cautious commander of the *San Pedro,* discussed the matter. "Two thousand miles," they said, "and maybe a trifle more. No man could estimate our daily rate of progress while we were fighting those wretched Machiparoans."

There was something hateful about the Omaguan village, and the Spaniards were glad to leave it. A kind of moss grew from the branches of high trees, and the superstitious men, looking at these dangling masses, declared that it reminded them of funeral crape. The huts were small and dark, the natural resting place for blood-sucking bats, giant ants, and tiny insects which burrowed into men's toes and caused painful swellings. There were wicked little snakes and bloated gray toads, and an atmosphere of hatred and loneliness. Neither Panama nor Number Five would sleep in the village. They declared that evil ghosts haunted the place, and they always took themselves off to the boats after they had seen to Orellana's comfort for the night.

Orellana and his men traveled another fifty miles down the river, skirmishing most of the way. Having gone only this short distance from the unpleasant Omaguan village, the men were surprised to come upon one of the prettiest villages they had seen during the voyage. The houses were high and slender and surrounded by verandas with floors of beaten earth. Great scarlet and white flowers blossomed along the bank of the river. There were neat hedges and well-kept gardens, and the turtle ponds were the best constructed the voyagers had seen.

"This is as fair a village as any in Spain," they declared. "In a place like this, a man might dream his whole life away in idle contentment. Let us hope the inhabitants are as peaceful as their home."

The Indians in the village were nothing of the sort. Their slingstones rattled and clanged against Orellana's mail when he rose to speak to them in his usual quiet and friendly voice. A hurtling javelin drove deep into the *Victoria's* planks. Another almost ended poor Father Vera's earthly existence, for it missed the good man's throat by a couple of inches and gave him a terrible fright.

Orellana made a hopeless gesture. He

glanced at his companions in the *Victoria*. "There are no women or children in sight," he said. "It is a sign that these people mean to attack. Kill no more of them than necessary, for dead bodies are not fitting in this pleasant village."

His men paid little attention to the order. Few of them, alas, were as merciful as their leader. All of them were embittered by memories of their recent furious struggle with the Machiparoans. They stabbed and struck and killed with fury when the first wave of villagers rushed down on them. The fight ended quickly. Fifty Indians lay dead on the grassy slope The rest disappeared into the forest.

These villagers had fought to protect more than their homes and plantations. In their huts were hundreds of beautiful vases made from local clay. Some of these vases were as exquisite as any from the potteries of Spain, and they were colored in delicate shades of pink, pale blue, and green.

Silently, and with a feeling of great sadness, a group of Orellana's officers crowded into the houses to gaze with wonder at these lovely jars and beakers and vases. Among these Spaniards were men who loved and appreciated fine art.

"Had we but known," they muttered regretfully, "we would not have fought against such artists. It would have been better to leave this village astern of us and encamp in the jungle. One should not strive to destroy a people who can create great beauty with their hands. It was thus that Spain lost many of the finest and most skilled craftsmen among the Indians of Mexico and Peru. Now we, too, have erred in similar manner."

"At least we will keep some of these larger vessels," said Orellana. "One day our countrymen may marvel at the skill and beauty with which they were made. Carry a few of the largest to the brigantines. They will serve as food containers during the rest of our voyage."

Another Spaniard, Balthazar Osorio, died that night from a stab wound in the neck. Orellana's party now consisted of himself, forty-five soldiers, Father Carvajal and Father Vera, and the two Negroes. Since the time the party had left Pizarro at the end of December, five months earlier, ten Spaniards had died of fever, wounds, or sickness.

There was plenty of food in that village of craftsmen. The men loaded the brigantines with quantities of dried maize, turtle meat coarsely ground flour, leaf-wrapped bunches of sun-dried bananas, and jars of palm oil. The vessels lumbered heavily down the river. A mile farther downstream, the water grew rough and eddying from the river's junction with another tributary. From then on, the width of the mighty stream increased so greatly that the men could no longer see from one bank to another.

"The more distant our enemies are, the better we will sleep at night," said Orellana. "With thirty of us wounded, we must travel for a while in midstream. It would only encourage the Indians to attack us more fiercely if they saw how weak we are."

The two boats went on down the river without sighting land for many hours at a time. It grew colder when the sun set, and the men slept under whatever coverings they could find. A steersman and a couple of sentinels remained awake in the starlit darkness, for it was impossible to be sure that some Indian fleet of canoes would not attack at night. The breeze was coming from the east again, and the high square sail in each brigantine carried the boats along swiftly while their occupants slept.

Food began to run short at the end of the

first week in June. "We must steer for land," said Orellana. "I pray Heaven we have left our enemies behind."

They sighted a large village on the northern shore. The inhabitants fled into the jungle without attempting to fight. Apparently the upriver drums had not warned them that the Spaniards were coming. Orellana and his armed party of men walked ashore without trouble and managed to capture a young Indian.

In this large, well-kept village they discovered a high and airy storehouse, with walls of split bamboo and a roof of thatched straw. The building was filled with wooden racks from floor to ceiling, on which hung beautifully woven capes. The outer side of each of these garments was exquisitely patterned with soft and many-colored plumage from unknown birds. In Europe robes such as these would have been priceless.

"What are they for?" Orellana asked the Indian prisoner. "Who wears such fine clothes in these regions?"

"They are for the Conori women who live farther down the river," the young man replied in a sulky voice. "My tribe makes all these cloaks for them in return for gold and silver and blocks of salt."

Some of the Spaniards laughed. "And these Conori women are the dreaded fighters of whom we have heard so much two thousand miles upstream? Perhaps we should arrive in their country bearing posies and with our clothes neatly mended."

Orellana translated these remarks. The Indian became sulkier and peered at the Spaniards through a tangle of dark hair hanging over his forehead. "Laugh now," he said. "Soon you will meet the Conori women and your laughter will turn to tears."

Orellana smiled and gave the young man a pat on his bare shoulder. "Here," he said, "take these as presents. Go in your canoe and tell the Conori women that soon we will have the pleasure of visiting their country." He placed a few beads and a mirror in the young Indian's hand.

The rest of the Spaniards, feeling annoyed that a heathen savage should speak to them so boldly, watched moodily as he paddled away downstream. Possibly the man did as Orellana said; perhaps he went no farther than around the next bend of the river. But that night, the dark recesses of the jungle throbbed and echoed with the sharp rattle of small wooden drums, whose notes carried an extraordinary distance. News of the coming of the boats was being flashed down the river again. The Spaniards, listening in their huts to the harsh clatter, fidgeted a little and wondered uneasily why the Conori women were so feared.

The current of the river seemed to change. The *Victoria* and the *San Pedro* were being carried close to the shore instead of cruising along far from land. They sighted villages every few miles, and noted that the forests seemed less luxuriant than those farther upstream. The groves of trees were lower, and fewer lianas looped and dangled from their upper branches. Even the houses were different. Most of them were built with white clay walls and had roofs of yellow straw. Some of these villages were curiously European in appearance.

"What kind of country are we coming to?" the Spaniards asked themselves. "Though these people shake their spears and howl insults at us as furiously as the other Indians did, they are no longer like the wild and primitive tribes we met upstream. Their houses are orderly and their gardens neat."

Orellana made one of his few mistakes. Curiosity tempted him to lead the two boats to the shore at a particularly large village, where several hundred armed warriors were assembled along the bank. When he called a greeting to them, they were unable to understand the dialect he spoke. The boats touched land, and the Indians came roaring down the bank in an irresistible attack.

The Spaniards were thrown back into their brigantines almost before they stepped out of them. Domiguez Miradero, the young Spaniard who sailed small boats for pleasure, was struck senseless by a heavy club. He fell face forward into the water and almost drowned before his comrades could lift him up. Parties of warriors kept up an unceasing shower of stones from their slings, and the heavy pebbles clanged against the Spaniards' mail with such force that the tempered steel was dented. Women and girls remained in the background of the fight instead of disappearing into the forest. They kept the slingers equipped with stones, brought fresh weapons to warriors whose weapons had been cut by Spanish swords, and kept up a shrill chanting to encourage their menfolk.

Somehow the Spaniards got the boats away from the bank. Breathless, bruised, and bleeding, they paddled hastily toward midstream. "*Dios!*" they gasped. "What sort of devils were those? They fought us as if Satan himself were urging them on. See how their spears have driven into this planking."

The men were bad-tempered and flustered after their defeat. Their conduct in the brigantines became almost mutinous. They argued about taking turns to row, grumbled at having to swab the boats clear of blood, and complained maliciously about the poor quality of the rations they were given to eat. They were proud men, and intensely vain of their skill with sword, crossbow, and arquebus. It hurt their pride to remember how a rabble of river savages had almost destroyed them.

That night Orellana spoke very firmly to the men as they moped around the fireside on a deserted islet in midstream. "It is I who must take the blame for what happened today," he said. "But at least all of us are still alive, and for that we should be thankful. We will gain nothing by bitterness and slovenly behavior.

If our discipline becomes slack now, how can we fight properly when some tribe attacks us again? The present conduct of some of us is like a worm in timber, or a rotten patch in an apple. It will poison the valiant courage you have shown up to the present. . . . What is it you are muttering, friend Aguilar?"

"Captain, I merely remarked that sour faces such as ours will scarcely please the Conori women," Benito de Aguilar replied with a grin.

The grim mood of the Spaniards suddenly vanished. Chuckling, they peered at one another's ragged beards and bandaged heads; at wounds wrapped in clumsy folds of blood-stained cloth, and feet ill protected by roughly made sandals.

Their chuckles became loud laughs, and Orellana himself began to smile. "Aye," he said. "As gentlemen and soldiers of Spain, we have a reputation for gallant appearance to maintain. From now on, we must do our best to maintain our country's honor as regards our dress. I, for one, will order Panama to clip my overlong hair with a dagger tonight."

So ended the second week of June in that year of 1542. After six months of rowing and fighting, raiding and starving, Orellana and his men had traveled three thousand miles down this unknown river, to which they had given the name *Marañon*.

That night, Diego Bermudez dreamed of a sunlit ocean, and young Alonso de Cabrera declared that he heard a sea bird cry overhead at midnight. No doubt he was wrong, but at least the news heartened his companions.

Orellana chose his villages more carefully after the last experience. The brigantines avoided the larger settlements and tried to remain out of sight of land as much as possible. Usually they approached the shore only when twilight was coming, so that it would be possible to elude a pursuing Indian fleet in the approaching darkness.

All the tribes along this stretch of river were utterly hostile. Possibly they had heard rumors of the white men's coming to the West Indies, and of how those pale-skinned strangers had massacred the Carib people of Hispaniola (Haiti) and Cuba. At any rate, Orellana and his men found no more friends like Aparia or Delicola. They had to fight wherever they set foot on land, and kill a dozen Indians for every bag of maize they wrenched from a plantation.

Once they were forced to set fire to a whole village before they could drive out the warriors lurking inside the huts. It was only when the flames died down, and black smoke was curling through the ruins, that the Spaniards discovered the bodies of fifty men lying in one of the largest huts. These unfortunate Indians had died in the flames rather than surrender to their attackers or escape into the forest.

During that particular fight, the Spaniards took only one prisoner, a young Indian girl. At first she struggled to escape; but when Orellana spoke to her in a language she understood, she became quiet and friendly. "There are men like yourselves living in the forests far to the north of this river," she said. "They have white bodies and black hair on their chins. I have heard that they were captured from a great ship which was wrecked somewhere near the River-Without-Banks. They were not killed, because they were most valiant fighters. Afterward they were adopted by various tribes, and married Indian wives. If you will trust me to be your guide, I can take you to the country where these men live."

Orellana hesitated. He yearned to meet these shipwrecked fellow Spaniards, but he could not risk a march through the jungle. A strong rear party would have to be left to guard the boats, which would mean that not more than twenty men could go with him. Twenty men were too few in a hostile country such as this.

"No," he said. "One day perhaps I shall return with larger ships and more men. For the present, we will remain on the river, and you will come with us to help me speak to other warriors who wish to fight against us."

The girl stepped aboard the *Victoria* without fear. "I am curious to learn how so few of you have managed to come so far down the river," she said. "Perhaps I shall learn your secret."

"You think there will be more fighting soon?" Orellana asked her.

The girl nodded calmly. "Of course," she said. "Four days' journey downstream from here, you will come to the tribes who fight under the orders of the Conori women. If you ventured into the land of these women on foot, all of you would most certainly die. They are the greatest fighters in this whole country. Even though you remain in your boats, I think you are going to die very soon."

A fleet of canoes was awaiting the coming of

the *Victoria* and the *San Pedro*. The long line of black-hulled vessels, each containing forty or fifty men, lay in midstream. As soon as the brigantines appeared in sight at dawn, the canoes raced forward in line to meet them. Several hundred bore down on the brigantines, and to avoid their being surrounded in mid-river, Orellana ordered the boats to be steered toward the northern shore.

"A wild boar attacked by dogs seeks to place its back against a tree so that it can face its enemies," he said. "We will have to do the same. Once our boats lie close to the bank, those canoes can only come directly at us."

The men at the oars pulled as quickly as they could. Slowly the *San Pedro* and the *Victoria* lumbered toward the rolling mass of forest, which reached almost to the shore. After them came the canoes. They had spread out in a great semicircle, hoping to surround the brigantines before the Spaniards reached the bank. The warriors were chanting and shouting, blowing blasts on wooden trumpets, and beating time for their paddlers on deep-toned gongs and drums.

The Spaniards hastily began buckling their breastplates, chin guards, and the straps which

secured their helmets. Arquebusiers lit the slow
fuses of their weapons; crossbowmen wound
back their steel springs and placed copper-
tipped bolts in the firing grooves. Only nine
men were equipped with long-distance weapons. There was no hope that they alone could
hold back the canoes, unless the arquebusiers
with their roaring, fire-spouting weapons caused
panic as well as casualties among the oncoming canoes.

The crash of these firearms produced the effect that Orellana was praying for. Several
Indians fell dead or wounded before the leaden
bullets, and the attacking warriors paused in
sudden alarm. The crossbowmen neatly shot
several of the leaders, who were easily recog-
nizable by their high feathered headdresses and
barbaric necklaces.

The arquebusiers reloaded before the enemy
flotilla came surging forward again. Their second volley caused a fresh delay, and the Indians' shouts of exultation changed to cries of
alarm and pain.

"Make for the village," Orellana called to
Diego Bermudez, who was at the *Victoria's*
steering oar. "We will strike right at the
enemy's heart."

The village lay within two hundred yards of the river. Nearly five hundred high, graceful houses stretched along the wooded shore for a distance of more than a mile. All these cottages had steeply slanted roofs which were thatched with straw. The eaves projected several feet beyond the walls to form low and shady verandas, supported by slender lengths of palm timber.

Hundreds of almost naked warriors began running along the shore to the village when they realized that the brigantines were aiming directly toward it. At least a thousand other warriors were already gathered in front of the houses. They stood in reasonably disciplined ranks which reached from the yellowish-brown mud of the landing place back to the village itself.

Orellana looked at this army in surprise. He glanced at his companions' tense and worried faces. "They have discipline," he said. "Someone who knows how soldiers should fight has trained them well. This will be a new and perhaps unpleasant experience for us, *compañeros*."

The *Victoria* was only fifty yards from the bank when a tall, light-skinned figure appeared suddenly in front of the dark ranks of the Indians. The Spaniards gasped with surprise when they saw a woman with a mass of tightly braided hair, and a splendid cloak of plumage clasped round her neck. Swinging up her mighty bow, she drew it back with a swift, powerful movement, and released the cord.

The heavy shaft came fast and true. It struck the *Victoria's* planking with a tremendous crack. The point drove right through the wood, and a Spaniard shouted with pain as the arrow pierced his unprotected leg.

Orellana looked with his one good eye from the splendid figure of the distant woman to the astonishing effect of her first shot. An expression almost of amusement spread across his lean, reddish-brown face. "Gentlemen," he said. "It appears that we are about to have the pleasure of meeting the Conori women. The first of them has demonstrated her prowess in a way that no man alive could hope to better."

Chapter Nine

The Conori Women

THE Spaniards who took part in the battle that followed never forgot the horror of it for the rest of their lives.

A shrieking mass of club-swinging, stabbing Indians rushed forward as the Spaniards climbed over the thwarts of the boats and began to wade ashore. The warriors seemed to know by instinct how best to attack their well-protected enemy. They lunged with their spears at the exposed legs and faces of the

Spaniards, or brought their clubs crashing down on knees and elbows, where there were joints in their opponents' armor. Even when a sword had pierced him, an Indian would try to drag his slayer down with him by throwing his arms around the steel-encased body. Spaniards were dazed and stunned by blows before they reached the shore, and were left to choke and flounder miserably in the muddy water which closed over their heads. When they tried to crawl to the beach, other warriors hit them again, or leaped onto their backs and forced their heads below the surface.

Orellana was knocked down, rose to his feet at once, and was struck on the head with such force that he fell to his knees again. While five or six of the Conori women, fighting with silent and deadly fury, led fresh parties of Indians to the attack, several other women stood slightly apart, sending arrow after arrow into the massed ranks of the confused Spaniards. Most of these arrows were turned aside by good steel armor, but others struck vulnerable spots. The courageous Father Carvajal, standing erect in the *Victoria* to call down the blessings of Heaven on his fighting countrymen, fell backward with an arrow protruding from between his ribs. Thin, white-faced Father Vera at once took the place of his stricken fellow priest, and no one could laugh scornfully at him because his thin voice quavered as he prayed aloud in Latin above the monstrous uproar of battle. An arrow struck Alonso de Cabrera's helmet with such force that he was temporarily blinded and had to be almost carried back to the nearer brigantine. Another arrow hit Juan Arnalte in the middle of his chest, which he had left uncovered by an *escaupile,* or cotton jacket. The shaft pierced his steel breastplate and plunged deeply into his chest. Although Arnalte continued to fight, he did so with blood running from his mouth and nose, knowing that he had received a fatal wound, yet unwilling to leave his encircled companions.

A young and handsome Conori woman came racing toward the *San Pedro,* at the head of a party of warriors. The four Spaniards guarding the brigantine were all wounded men, and besides them there remained only the two Negroes. Little Panama, trying valiantly to face the onrush, went down under a terrible stroke from the woman's heavy bow, with blood pouring from his head. Number Five seized a fallen club, killed two Indians with it, and succeeded in dragging his friend's body into the center of the boat. The four injured Spaniards lined the thwarts and fought harder than they had ever fought in their lives, knowing that nothing but death was facing them.

Orellana glanced back at the river and saw that the *San Pedro* was in great danger of being overwhelmed. "Arquebusiers and crossbowmen return to the brigantine," he shouted. "Aim at the women. Leave the warriors to us."

The men did as they were ordered. Swiftly they cleared the *San Pedro* of attackers. But even in the midst of this wild fighting they muttered hoarse, shamefaced prayers, asking Providence for forgiveness. Hard and ruthless soldiers though they were, the idea of killing women was something they loathed and despised. Their hands moved uneasily on arquebus and crossbow. Although they fired constantly at the Conori women ashore, they failed to kill all of them. The survivors fought on, using their bows or spears as savagely as the warrior men under their command. When any of the Indians seemed likely to give way, the women struck at them ferociously and drove them back into the fight.

The Spaniards never reached the village. Indeed, they could not advance more than thirty yards from the beach. Fresh waves of Indians rolled down on them like the tempestuous surges of an angry ocean. The warriors sprang or climbed over the piled bodies of their dead countrymen in their unceasing drive to get at Orellana and his men. In the forefront all the while, the Conori women fought with the unyielding, silent ferocity of jungle tigers.

At the end of an hour's fighting, Orellana knew he could never hold that littered and bloodstained beach. He gave the order to return to the brigantines; and the men began to retreat backward, fighting off the enemy as they went. Those who were first to reach the boats pushed the craft into deeper water and steadied them while the others clambered aboard.

The Indians waded out to pursue the retreating Spaniards. They tried to drag armor-clad men back into the water, where the weight of their mail would eventually drown them. This was a death that the Spaniards naturally feared more than any other. Wild and terrible fighting took place alongside the boats before the oarsmen hurriedly rowed them away from the bank. Yet even now the battle was not ended. The Indians would not leave the wounded and

exhausted Spaniards alone. The canoes that were still out in the river came sweeping shoreward and formed a circle around the retreating boats.

The *Victoria* was the first to burst through this ring, with arquebuses roaring and crossbows twanging their deadly song. After her came the smaller *San Pedro,* in which Spaniards were fighting hand-to-hand duels with daring warriors who had actually leaped aboard her. The two boats lumbered onward, their rowers gasping from exhaustion or moaning with the pain of their wounds.

The canoes did not follow the brigantines. They paddled shoreward to the spot where a great crowd of warriors gathered silently around the bodies of seven Conori women who had led them with valor and ferocity. Meanwhile, the young Indian girl who had wished to see how the Spaniards would fare in this river battle lay dead in the bottom of the *Victoria.* She had been killed outright by an arrow fired from the shore.

All that afternoon the two brigantines drifted uncontrolled down the sunny river. The arrow had been withdrawn from Father Carvajal's body and the wound clumsily bandaged, but

he was near death. Juan Arnalte finally died
and his body was slipped overside. Nearly
every Spaniard was bleeding from wounds, and
some were so exhausted by loss of blood that
they lay like dead men in the boats. Those
who had rowed the brigantine away from the
shore had spent the last of their strength in
doing so. Now they sprawled on the seats, too
dazed to take another stroke.

Late that afternoon, when the golden sun
was sinking behind the western forest, Orellana stirred and sat up. "The river has been
carrying us along at four miles an hour," he
muttered. "We have come fifteen or twenty
miles from the place where we fought. Let us
make for the grassy little beach yonder, where
we can rest more comfortably and tend our
wounds better."

There was no sign of any warriors among the
red-and-yellow-flowered bushes which fringed
the little clearing. Yet as the boats were
beached side by side, a rain of slender, black
arrows came humming toward the startled
crews. After the arrows came a wave of charging Indians.

Almost before the Spaniards were ashore,
they were being forced back to the boats. A

second arrow struck Father Carvajal. This time the missile entered one of his eyes and stayed there. The warriors came leaping through the shallow water and tried to climb aboard the brigantines. Even the most badly wounded Spaniards had to struggle to their feet and help drive them off.

Once more the rowers swung their boats away from that hostile shore and headed back to midstream. "We'll cross to the southern bank," said Orellana. "There'll be no rest for us on this northern shore tonight. Every warrior in the country is waiting for us. We may find peace on the other side of the river, where the villages are smaller and farther apart. I will take an oar. Let those who have strength row with me."

The brigantines reached the dark shadows of the southern bank long after the moon had risen above the forest. The men made no fires and cooked no food. They stumbled ashore, spread cloaks and blankets on the dew-wet grass, and fell down upon them. All that night they slept uneasily, while wounded companions muttered in pain, and others sobbed in terror with nightmare memories of the fight.

* * * * * * * *

A young Indian had been captured in one
of the battles. During the next two days, Orellana spoke with him for hours at a time. Every
now and then he paused to write down a new
word in his vocabularies, or to repeat a phrase
to make sure he had heard it correctly. He
asked the prisoner many questions about the
warrior women. "Who are these Conori
women?" he asked. "Where do they live? Do
they have husbands like other women? How
do they learn to fight so fiercely?"

"Their country is not far inland from this
river," the prisoner answered. "A man could
walk there in perhaps three days. The women
live alone, ruled over by their Queen, Conori.
They build good houses of stone or wood for
themselves, and are very skilled in spinning
cotton and in the making of silver ornaments.
All their young girls are taught to fight with
weapons, like men, and they live hard, active
lives. They grow up strong and beautiful, like
the women you saw. Sometimes the Conori
women kidnap husbands for themselves when
they make war against another tribe. But these
husbands are not allowed to stay long in the
country of the women. They are sent back
to their own lands. I have heard that male chil-

dren are always killed and only female ones allowed to live. All other tribes along the river are greatly afraid of Queen Conori and her women warriors, and even our most powerful chieftains dare not enter her country unless the Queen gives them permission. The tribe you fought against is friendly with the Conori women and is led by them in war. If you and your friends entered the land of the Queen, you would certainly all be killed, for there are many hundreds of these women."

Orellana considered all this news. "If you had told me such a story before we saw the Conori women for ourselves," he answered, "I would have said you were a great liar or a madman. But now I can believe what you say, for these women are truly the greatest fighters we have met during our voyage down this river."

"Pray Heaven we have left them behind for good," muttered the men in the *Victoria*. "We have no wish to encounter such beautiful devils again."

Orellana translated the remarks, and the Spaniards anxiously awaited an answer.

The Indian shook his head. "You have left the Conori and their friendly tribes behind," he said. "There will be much mourning in the country now. Never before have seven Conori women been killed in one battle, and we were sure that no one could face them as you have done."

For several days, Orellana kept the boats out in midstream and only ventured near the southern shore when twilight was approaching. Father Carvajal was still alive. The surprised Spaniards declared that it was because he was a holy man, and therefore helped by Providence. "If any of us were wounded as severely," they said, "our bones would be resting on the bed of the river by now. Yet the good Father has been wounded *twice* and still survives. . . . Aye, and he is even showing signs of temper. Did he not scold poor Father Vera this morning for pouring too much oil into his wounds?"

At the end of a week, Orellana swung the boats back to the northern side of the river. His companions exclaimed in amazement when they saw the jungle they had known for so long was disappearing. Instead of an unending line of forest, they saw soft green hills, open fields, and villages set in the middle of fine plantations.

"Perhaps the temper of the people has improved with their country," murmured Orellana. "This time I leave the verdict to you, *compañeros*. Shall we risk visiting that shore, or shall we remain here in midstream?"

"Let us approach it cautiously," the men answered. "If the people show any sign of fight, we can refrain from landing. But if they are friendly, it will be a chance for us to procure some decent food again. For a whole week now we have eaten little but parrot flesh—which is sweet but unsatisfying—and fish which taste mostly of river mud."

The Indian prisoner was more cautious. "A black-skinned people live in this region," he said. "I know nothing about them except that they usually attack anyone who comes near their villages."

The Indians were hostile, yet they fought in such a cautious manner that the Spaniards were able to wade ashore and search the first little village they reached for supplies of food. The black-skinned warriors stayed at a distance and fired slender little arrows from almost toylike bows. The Spaniards, confident of their good armor, laughed and paid small attention to these arrows. Only once or twice did they have to beat back an attack made with spears and clubs which were lighter and less dangerous than those of other tribes. They returned to their boats, laden with maize, yams, wild honey, and the dried flesh of peccaries, all of which they found in the huts.

Those arrows were not as harmless as they seemed. That night, Antonio de Carranza became delirious. He lay babbling in the *Victoria;* and one of his legs, which had been slightly grazed by an arrow, swelled up and turned black.

"Poison," said the Indian prisoner. "It is prepared from a kind of vine which grows in the forest. Your friend will die."

The Spaniards dropped Carranza's body overside at dawn the next morning. Frightened and silent, they went on rowing down the middle of the river. None of them had any wish to go ashore until it was necessary to find more food for themselves. They had never feared enemies who fought with clean weapons, but these poison arrows of the Negro people frightened them. Carranza's death had been a terrible one, and all the Spaniards prayed devoutly that they might avoid a similar fate.

Orellana spent the day in silent thought. His

face was hard and anxious, so the men left him alone. Shortly before sunset, he spoke for the first time. "We will land there," he said, nodding to a palm-dotted islet which lay directly ahead. "We would be foolish to go any farther without heightening the sides of our brigantines to give us more protection from arrows."

The boats rested on the beach for two days, while Mexia and his companions felled palm trees and sawed lengths of soft, springy planking. When this timber had been nailed along the thwarts, the seated rowers were under cover. Men standing erect in the boats, however, could still see over the top of the bulwarks.

During the time spent on this islet, the Spaniards clumsily split open green coconuts and drank the sweet liquid inside. Older and riper nuts provided them with firm white kernels which were pleasant to eat and satisfied their hunger. Carelessly they tossed the green-husked shells in the direction of the river. Their action helped keen-eyed Diego Bermudez to make a happy discovery. He stood looking at several discarded coconuts and from them to the nearby water. "Comrades," he said presently. "I think we are near the sea."

The Spaniards, Orellana among them, stared at him with delighted surprise on their haggard faces. "Why do you think so?" they demanded.

Diego pointed to the coconut husks. "See these. A while ago I happened to notice that some of them had rolled to the edge of the water. Now they are several feet away from it, yet no one has moved them. Therefore, I think the river is receding. If my guess is right, the water will return to these coconuts before nightfall."

All that long hot afternoon, the men kept looking up from their work on the boats to see if the river was returning. They crowded to the water's edge when the first of the big green nuts went floating away from the shore, bobbing and twisting on the gliding current. They knew then that Diego was right; they had reached the tidal waters of the river.

Feeling rested and encouraged, the crew of the brigantines rowed swiftly away from the islet. Longingly they glanced up at the glittering blue sky, hoping vainly to see clouds that might bring a breeze with them. But no wind came that day, and they were forced to labor at their oars until sundown, when they camped for the night on another islet.

Negro warriors found them soon after dawn the following day. Big canoes came flying across the river toward the brigantines. A number of them ran alongside the *San Pedro*, and savages tried to leap aboard. The boat's heightened sides made this very difficult for them. As fast as a warrior appeared on top of the bulwarks, a lunging sword or a sharp-pointed pike sent him toppling back into deep water.

But other canoes hovered at a distance, and from them came whispering showers of those slender little arrows, one scratch from which meant death.

The Spaniards were wearing all the armor they owned, including greaves to protect their lower legs, steel gloves, and leather face guards. Yet as they fought the Indians climbing aboard, they were constantly worried by the sound of those wicked arrows smacking against the timbers of the boats.

The fight lasted from sunrise until halfway through the morning. All that time, canoes and brigantines went drifting down the river, to the accompaniment of roaring explosions from the arquebuses, yells from the Indians, and the battle cries of the Spaniards.

The canoes were beaten off, and a hundred

of the warriors were killed. The rest paddled away to the distant shore, where an enormous and excited crowd had gathered to watch the fight. As Orellana's men rowed hastily out to midstream, they sighted astern of their boats high blue hills and an open countryside dotted with noble groves of forest.

An arrow had scratched Garcia de Soria, a young man of good family. "I longed to smell the fresh breeze of the ocean again," he said to his grieving friends. "I was born on the Spanish coast, overlooking the Bay of Biscay; and I would like to leave this world within sound of the Atlantic Ocean. But the pain is spreading through my body already, and I shall not live to hear the sea again."

Garcia died that evening. They buried him in a lonely forest glade on the southern bank of the river. That was the last time Orellana and his men camped and slept on the shores of the Amazon River, which they called the Marañon. At last they had almost reached the sea.

Chapter Ten

Isles of the Caribs

THE boats glided onward in the morning sunshine. Now there was no sign of the mainland on either side, for the river had rapidly increased its width to a hundred miles. Yet there were patches of dry ground all around the brigantines. As the heat of the sun increased, the Spaniards saw palm-covered islands looming up through the warm white mist. Meadows of soft green grass reached almost to the shores; and there were glades of flowering bushes, where birds chirped and fluttered in the sunshine. Along the white sand of the beaches were wavy black lines formed by dead and drifting vegetation. The Spaniards gazed at these high-water marks and smiled with relief. "Diego Bermudez was right," they said. "We are nearing the sea, and the tide grows mightier with every mile we advance. Yet the water overside is as sweet to the taste as it was a thousand miles upstream."

"Doubtless it will remain so until long after we have left the coast behind," Orellana replied. "A great river like this runs far into the ocean before it becomes salty. But I think we must make camp at one of these islands ahead of us. Our boats must be checked, for the last time, by our good friend Diego Mexia, to whom we already owe so much."

A warm westerly breeze came booming down the river. The Spaniards hoisted the sails and went flying past the shores of scattered islands. As the wind strengthened, it roughened the surface of the water. The brigantines began bumping and pitching across waves of considerable size, and flying spray soaked the men aboard them.

"We'd do well to land as soon as possible,

Captain," suggested Diego Mexia. "The boats have come a long way. I cannot be sure that their timbers are still sound. What's more, I never designed them to ride seas like these."

The smaller islands were uninhabited, but on the larger ones lived men and women of the Carib nation. They were short, burly, sullen people, with slanting black eyes and broad faces. Their skins were a dark reddish-brown, and were smeared with red, white, and blue ocher. The Spaniards recognized them at once; they had seen other Caribs in the West Indian islands.

"We'll leave them alone," Orellana said cautiously. "They're dangerous fighters, as some of our countrymen have discovered to their pain and sorrow. If we land on a deserted island, they may decide we intend no harm and leave us alone. All the saints in heaven will witness the truth of my words when I declare I have no wish to do any more fighting."

Increasing hunger made the Spaniards reluctant to listen to their leader's good advice. They craved meat and fish and vegetables instead of coconut kernels, which was all that the smaller and uninhabited islands could supply in the way of food. When the crew of the

San Pedro saw a little village standing close to the shore, they loudly demanded permission to search the houses for supplies.

Orellana shrugged his lean shoulders and agreed. Borne by the swift current, and with a steady breeze filling their sails, the *Victoria* and the *San Pedro* altered course until their bows were directly pointed at the cluster of thatched and wooden-walled houses.

The *Victoria* grounded on the beach safely. But the *San Pedro* struck a submerged log several yards from shore. One of her bottom planks was ripped out, and she became waterlogged within a minute.

Orellana glanced at the men wading ashore in water that reached to their necks. Carib warriors were gathering from all directions. Several hundred of them had already assembled in front of the houses and were getting ready to charge.

"We must hold these Caribs back from the boats," he said. "Diego Mexia, take the two Negroes and any other men you need. See how quickly you can beach the *San Pedro* and mend her broken plank. Our lives depend on the swiftness of your hammer and the sharpness of your saw."

A wave of Caribs came racing down the beach. They surrounded the group of armor-clad men and almost overwhelmed them with their spears. The weak, hungry, and exhausted Spaniards, most of whom were suffering from half-healed wounds, fought with weary desperation. They were determined not to die so near the end of their voyage, yet inwardly they wondered how long they could resist these powerful, reckless Caribs, who fought with such uncontrollable fury and cunning.

Lanky Diego Mexia was a man who liked to take his time and make his measurements with care. Yet no sooner had his helpers hauled the damaged *San Pedro* onto the beach then he began working at a speed that astounded them. Instead of pausing to select a nail with care, or to handle a chisel thoughtfully before using it, he toiled with the utmost haste. The loud banging of his hammer was drowned by the uproar of battle, and the rasp of his saw was lost in the cries of the savages.

An hour after he had begun mending the *San Pedro*, Mexia thrust his way through the Caribs surrounding Orellana, using an ax to clear a path for himself. "She'll float," he said. "I'll say no more than that."

Orellana's anxious face became calmer. "Since we came here to get food, we will not leave without it. Get the boats afloat and guard them until we return." Raising his voice, Orellana shouted, "Forward, comrades. Drive them back to their village. One last effort for the honor of Spain and our king."

The Spaniards began to move forward, driving the Caribs before them. They reached the houses; and while half of them held off the furious warriors, the other half burst into the huts and seized whatever food they could find. Clutching bundles of dried fish and smoked haunches of jungle pig, and carrying sacks of maize and great clusters of bananas over their shoulders, they came hurrying out of the huts to rejoin their comrades. Retreating backward, fighting as they went, the Spaniards returned to the river with their burdens. They hurled the food into the brigantines, then turned and drove back the Caribs who had followed them into the shallow water. Then they scrambled clumsily over the high sides of the brigantines and thrust the boats clear of the bank with their oars.

So ended the last day of July, 1542. That evening the Spaniards camped on an uninhab-

ited island. They boiled maize over hot but smokeless fires made from the dry midribs of palm fronds and driftwood. They were a morose crowd of men, with little to say to one another.

Young Alonso de Cabrera expressed the thoughts of the whole party when he said, half-jokingly, "After seven months of acting like a farmyard robber, I, for one, have eaten enough food secured by bloodshed and battle. Soon, please God, we will leave this river behind us. Until then, I prefer to eat coconuts, or whatever simple fare God may provide, rather than fill my stomach again with pilfered food. Those Caribs whom we met today were rightfully defending their homes and property against us."

That night, Alvar Gonzales died of wounds.

Forty-eight hours later, Diego Bermudez was certain he could smell the sea. "Nor am I mistaken," he said. "There is a cool and welcome saltiness in the breeze today. I have known the stinking vapors of jungle swamps too long not to know the difference now."

Orellana was inclined to believe Bermudez. "Then now is the time to strengthen the brigantines," he said. "On this piece of land we can cut sufficient timber and live well enough until our work is done. Unless misfortune comes to us again, the Caribs will not find our camp."

For the last time, Diego Mexia wearily got out his bag of tools. Saws and axes were sharpened, and the little forge was heated with charcoal left over from the building of the *Victoria*. All the men who were strong enough to work began to saw planks, make nails, and fell trees. Others such as Father Carvajal and Panama, who were still suffering from wounds, spent their time hunting for food or cooking the meager rations which still remained.

The little island was well wooded, with a variety of trees. This was lucky for the Spaniards, because Diego Mexia insisted on almost rebuilding the *San Pedro* and completely overhauling the *Victoria*. For all this work he needed different kinds of timber: one kind for the ribs, another for the planking, and a third for the half decks he intended to make for both brigantines. Having finished his work on the hulls, he set about making a pump for each boat. He built them from odd pieces of leather, forged lengths of iron, and from ingeniously shaped pieces of timber. Diego Bermudez, assisted by clever-handed Lorenzo Munoz, who knew not how to write his own name, and Dominguez Miradero, the young nobleman, began making stronger masts and sails.

All this work took two weeks to complete. The food taken from the Caribs was soon eaten, and the islet contained little in the way of natural supplies. The men were forced to live on coconuts, unripe plums, a few muddy-tasting fish they managed to catch in their nets, and land crabs. The latter lived in ratlike holes in the sand, and usually managed to reach these lairs long before they were caught. The Spaniards were compelled to dig in the sand with their hands, swords, and daggers to capture their prey. Their tempers grew short as their hunger increased.

"For heaven's sake, speed your work," they said angrily to Mexia and Bermudez. "One would think you intended to sail with the royal fleet of Spain, by the care you are taking with paint and cotton and resin. Until we are afloat again, we must continue to live on these few mouthfuls of miserable food, for which we must dig and burrow and scrape like a pack of wild dogs."

Diego Mexia grew bad-tempered when spoken to in this manner. Often he dropped the tools with which he was working and strode away to the beach to sit in sulky silence and gaze at the river.

But Diego Bermudez merely laughed at ill-tempered remarks. "Friends," he said, looking at the angry, impatient men with his clear blue eyes, "once we are out on the open sea, we will have no chance to strengthen the boats again. The work we do now must last until we reach Cuagua. I know how greatly a wild ocean may test the strength of a fine vessel new from a Spanish shipyard. These little boats of ours are nothing but toys for children on a lake."

At last the brigantines were launched again. They floated squarely in the water, and there was now an impression of strength about their sturdy decks and tapering masts. When the sails were hoisted, the brigantines sailed fast and easily. They shipped less water than formerly, and most of the men could find shelter under the low deck which covered the forward half of each boat. As quick to approve as they were to complain, the men congratulated Mexia and Bermudez on the improvements they had made.

The islands inhabited by the Caribs were left astern. Near the mouth of the river they came to other islands. A peaceful tribe of Indians lived on them. They seemed to have no weapons, and spent most of their time cultivating the land or fishing.

Orellana could manage to make himself understood by these people, for he had been studying the strange dialect spoken by the young Indian prisoner on board the *Victoria*. "Give us what food you can spare," he called to the men and women who had gathered on the beaches to gaze at the boats and the bearded men aboard them. "See. In return for your presents, I will give you mirrors and nails and brass bells."

The Indians smiled and went off to their plantations. They returned with baskets made of plaited coconut fronds, which were filled with big potatolike yams. Apparently they ate no meat, or perhaps they had none ready at the time.

"It is strange," Orellana said on the third day of this diet, "that however we cook yams, they always taste exactly the same. Except, perhaps, when we mix them with eels or crabs. Then they usually manage to taste a little worse."

On the twenty-fourth of August, the brigantines emerged from a channel which wound in and out past palm-covered islands. Orellana scanned the empty expanse of water ahead, which reached to the sunlit horizon. His wound-scarred face relaxed in a smile of relief. "Lower the sails," he said. "We must turn back to spend the night on one of the islands behind us, and collect whatever food we can find there. I think Diego Bermudez will agree with me that yonder lies the ocean. We have taken eight months to reach it, and have come perhaps four thousand miles. Alas that fourteen of our comrades are no longer with us to enjoy this splendid sight!"

Chapter Eleven

The Deep-Sea Voyage

THE coast line was out of sight astern when Diego Bermudez glanced up at the sun and pushed the tiller to starboard. The *Victoria* came heeling around and steadied on a north-westerly course. Astern of her, the *San Pedro* made a similar movement.

"If my memory is right, Captain, we are now running parallel to the shore," Diego called to Orellana. "We should sight land again before nightfall."

Orellana, his face pale from seasickness, nodded with approval. "With neither compass nor astrolabe to check our position, it is wiser to run parallel to the coast."

The two heavily laden brigantines scudded northward across the bright sea. The men lounged on the floor boards, where they were protected against the unusual coolness of the ocean breeze. Now they were in cheerful spirits. Despite the poor and scanty rations in the boats, and their spells of seasickness, the Spaniards felt that at last they had almost reached safety. Only 1200 miles to the northwest lay the Spanish island of Cuagua.

"Have we not already sailed four thousand miles down a hostile and fever-stricken river?" they asked one another. "Often we have had less to eat than we will have during the next two weeks. This voyage of ours across a clean and friendly sea is nothing but a holiday. These clay jars from the village of potters are full of drinking water, the wind is driving our boats along with excellent speed, we can sleep all day if we wish, and good Diego Bermudez is sure he can follow the coast all the way. Why, friends, we have nothing more to fear."

As it happened, Bermudez went a little

wrong in the course he was steering. By the time evening came, there was no sign of land to port. The Spaniards lay down to sleep feeling rather uneasy. They were thinking that storms often arose in these waters, and that the brigantines were very small craft in which to ride angry waves. Although they were daring soldiers on land, most Spaniards disliked and feared the open sea.

"What if Bermudez has mistaken the Marañon for another river?" they wondered. "Perhaps we are much farther south than he thinks, or the coast does not lie the way he says he remembers it."

They worried during the starlit hours of darkness, but when a pale dawn spread across the ocean, Diego Mexia sighted land again.

The *San Pedro* had lagged almost a mile astern of the *Victoria* during the night. Orellana was anxious about the little brigantine's slower speed. When the two boats came alongside each other, he ordered the men in the *San Pedro* to make an extra sail with blankets and to rearrange the loading of the cargo. After these things were done, her performance improved.

Orellana watched the progress of the two

vessels contentedly. "How long will it take us to reach Cuagua?" he asked Bermudez. "The wind is freshening from the south, and today we are making better speed."

Diego glanced at the foaming blue water alongside. "Twelve or thirteen days, Captain. But I have heard that in these waters there is sometimes a flat calm for a long while. I cannot make a definite guess. It all depends on the weather we find ahead."

That night the wind grew stronger. The *Victoria* began to heave and plunge alarmingly, banging and bouncing across the waves' fierce crests. Shivering men aboard her peered through the darkness, trying to catch a glimpse of the *San Pedro*.

They saw nothing. By morning, the wind had gone down only a little. Land was visible in the distance whenever the *Victoria* rose high enough on the tossing waves for her passengers to sight it, but there was no sign at all of the *San Pedro*.

All that day the *Victoria* sailed on alone. The thirty men aboard her were silent and depressed. They knew that the *San Pedro* was smaller and lighter than their own vessel. With sixteen men aboard her, she had perhaps been too heavily laden to face the night's gale. If she had foundered in the darkness, all those gallant comrades were drowned.

The wind went down that day and the sky cleared. Toward evening, an offshore breeze brought a heavy shower of rain. The Spaniards spread a sail to catch the pelting drops and carefully refilled their drinking jars. The total food for each man that day was a small piece of dried fish, a handful of maize soaked in water, and half a coconut. Yet such was their grief over the missing brigantine, that they forgot their usual harmless grumbling at having so little to eat.

Ten days went past. The *Victoria* still sailed on alone across an empty ocean. The southerly breeze came almost steadily, and the sun blazed down from a hot blue sky.

"We must watch for land ahead," Bermudez declared on the eleventh day. "By now we should be nearing the southern coast of the island of Trinidad. Would to Heaven that our countrymen had conquered and settled the place! As matters are, we must sail round the northern end of Trinidad to reach Cuagua. Between Trinidad and the mainland of South America lies a narrow strait which mariners

have named the Serpent's Mouth. Should our
boat be drawn into that strait, we might pass
too close to the island. If the Caribs see us,
they will attack in great swarms. They have no
liking for Spaniards."

Thereafter, the men took turns sitting on
the swaying deck of the *Victoria*, to watch the
distant northern horizon for the first sign of
land. Mournfully they thought of their lost
companions in the *San Pedro*. There were only
twenty-six fighting men in the *Victoria*. The
other passengers consisted of the two priests,
the Indian prisoner, Panama, and Number Five.
Several arquebusiers and crossbowmen were
in the *San Pedro*. An attack by the Caribs
would be a dangerous matter without the as-
sistance of these men. At this late stage of the
voyage the Spaniards were praying that they
need not risk their lives in combat again.

They sighted land that afternoon. Diego
Bermudez gazed at the distant blue mountains
rising mistily above the sea. "There is Trinidad," he said. "No, do not cheer so loudly, my
friends. Look out there toward the open sea.
The breeze is failing. I fear we may be drawn
into the Serpent's Mouth."

"Out oars," said Orellana sharply. "If our

sails will not carry us forward, we must rely on our muscles."

All that long, hot afternoon, the Spaniards pulled vigorously at the oars. The *Victoria* moved heavily across a calm and shining ocean, and the mountains drew nearer. By sunset, they were lying directly beyond the bow.

Diego Bermudez shook his head fearfully. "Captain, the tide is setting in through the Serpent's Mouth. It is drawing us with it. We will have to pass through the channel. We must pray that the Carib people do not sight our boat off their coast."

Father Carvajal, his head covered with bandages, rose to his feet and prayed long and heartily in Latin. A yellow twilight spread across the sky, and the calm sea continued to lap against the *Victoria's* clumsy hull. As it grew dark, the Spaniards spoke in whispers and peered anxiously at the black outline of mountains against a starlit sky.

A swift current urged the brigantine through the channel all that night. When daylight came, the Spaniards smiled thankfully to see the coast of Trinidad lying far astern.

"What now, good Diego?" asked Orellana. "How do we make for Cuagua from here?"

Bermudez remained silent for a moment, while he tried to recall the charts he had known in his seafaring days. "We are floating in the Gulf of Paria," he said presently. "Behind us, as you can see, lies Trinidad. To the west and south of us is the mainland. We must go northward to reach the open sea again, through a passage called the Mouths of the Dragon. When we are through that channel, we can sail westward to Cuagua without further trouble. We must row, Captain. I do not think a breeze will reach this sheltered gulf today."

Once again the men took turns at the heavy oars. They moved slowly northward to the open sea beyond the Mouths of the Dragon. Every now and then they glanced unhappily at the distant coast of Trinidad, wondering if some sharp-eyed Carib warrior had observed the *Victoria*.

A breeze from the north came just before twilight. The brigantine was forced southward again, back to where she had lain that morning. All the day's heavy labor was lost.

Next morning the Spaniards tried again. Before nightfall, they saw ahead of them a number of rocky little islets, which marked the entrance to the Mouths of the Dragon. In spite of aching muscles and empty stomachs, they managed to grin. "We'll reach the open sea by dawn tomorrow," they said. "Two days after that, we'll drink good red wine with our countrymen in Cuagua, and sleep on well-filled mattresses."

The northerly breeze came again that night. The *Victoria* drove southward before it. When morning came, the brigantine was once more at the southern end of the Gulf of Paria. The weather had changed, and warm, tropical rain was pouring down. The surface of the Gulf was covered with brownish waves, and the northern wind was still blowing.

"It is useless to break our backs with hours of rowing in this weather," said Orellana. "The mainland lies only a few miles astern of us. Let us camp there for the day."

The edge of the jungle was close to the shore. The Spaniards managed to kindle a smoky fire by pouring coconut oil on the rain-wet wood they had collected. They spent the day sleeping in damp shelter under the trees, or searching for something to eat. Coconut palms grew high above their heads, but no one was able to climb the slippery gray trunks to gather the heavy nuts. They were forced to chop down a tree to get them. They found no other food in that unfriendly forest.

The wind had gone down next morning and the sea was calm. By rowing all day, the Spaniards reached the southern end of the Mouths of the Dragon before sunset. They anchored for the night in the shelter of a barren hump of islet, using a cable plaited from lianas and a heavy lump of rock to hold their boat. They lay awake in terrible anxiety, praying they would not hear the approaching murmur of the northerly breeze.

The night was utterly calm and the sky full of stars. As soon as it was light enough to see any distance ahead, they began rowing again. Orellana spent his time gazing anxiously upward at the pale blue sky and thence to the twisting rock-strewn channel beyond the slowly moving boat.

The calm lasted all that day, and no breeze came at nightfall. The channel was widening out and the shoals were growing fewer.

"We must row until we reach the open sea," said Orellana. "It would be foolish to spend the night sleeping and thus risk losing what we have won during the past two days."

The *Victoria* edged into deep and open

water before morning. Her crew were too exhausted to cheer or to mutter more than a brief prayer of thankfulness. They pulled in their oars and fell asleep almost before the clumsy sails were hoisted. All that day they slept, hearing, as if in a dream, the swift lap of the sea and the steady murmur of a breeze in the clumsy rigging.

The low brown hump of land which men called the island of Cuagua rose above the horizon two days later. By noon, the *Victoria* was gliding into a rocky little harbor. The hungry men stared almost unbelievingly at white-walled Spanish houses on the low beach in front of them.

Orellana rose swiftly to his feet. He swung up an arm in greeting to a distant group of figures hurrying down to the water's edge. "Now God be thanked," he exclaimed. His scarred and bearded face was filled with delight. "Though we lost sight of her in that wild night storm, our little *San Pedro* came safely to land. See how eagerly our companions are hastening to greet us! It is a good end to our eight months' voyage down the Marañon River."

Epilogue

ORELLANA and his party left Captain Pizarro on the banks of the Amazon River in December, 1541. For three weeks Pizarro led his 250 men downstream, hoping to meet Orellana returning in the *San Pedro* with supplies of food. At the end of that time, hunger and exhaustion had reduced his men to the stage where they could go no farther.

Pizarro then decided to return to Quito. He and his men were lucky enough to discover a yucca plantation, where they obtained sufficient supplies to keep them alive for a while. However, before they had reached the foothills of the Cordilleras Mountains, they were absolutely starving. By that time they had killed and eaten all their horses and dogs, and were living on berries, roots, insects, and snakes. Their clothes were in utter rags, and most of the men were without shoes of any kind.

Out of the 250 men, only 80 crossed the mountain passes with Pizarro and reached Quito alive. The rest died during the journey.

Bad news was awaiting Pizarro in Quito. His elder brother, Francisco Pizarro, the Viceroy of Peru, had been murdered by a treacherous party of his own Spanish countrymen. A new viceroy named Vaca de Castro was now in power.

Gonzalo Pizarro promptly organized a rebellion against Vaca de Castro, defeated his army in battle, and forced Castro to escape from Peru. In 1548, six years after his return journey from the headwaters of the Amazon or Marañon River, Pizarro was in turn defeated in battle by a new viceroy of Peru named Pedro de la Gasca. He was taken prisoner and condemned to be beheaded. He died bravely on the scaffold in the forty-second year of his life.

RONALD SYME

Cook Islands, 1956